INTERLINKING OF INDIAN RIVERS

Published by
Lotus Press Publishers & Distributors

INTERLINKING OF INDIAN RIVERS

Radha Kant Bharati

Lotus PRESS

4735/22, Prakash Deep Building,
Ansari Road, Daryaganj,
New Delhi - 110002

Lotus Press Publishers & Distributors
Unit No. 220, 2nd Floor, 4735/22, Prakash Deep Building,
Ansari Road, Daryaganj, New Delhi- 110002
Ph: 098118-38000
E-mail : lotuspress1984@gmail.com
Visit us : www.lotuspress.co.in

Interlinking of Indian Rivers

ISBN: 978-81-8382-329-6
Second Revised Edition

Published by: **Lotus Press, Publishers & Distributors,** New Delhi- 2
Printed at: **Bharat Offset Works**, New Delhi

ए. बी. पंडया
A. B. Pandya
अध्यक्ष
Chairman

भारत सरकार
केन्द्रीय जल आयोग
जल संसाधन मंत्रालय
कमरा नं० 315 (द), सेवा भवन
आर. के. पुरम, नई दिल्ली-110066
Government of India
Central Water Commission
Ministry of Water Resources
Room No. 315 (S), Sewa Bhawan
R. K. Puram, New Delhi-110066

Forword

I have gone through the manuscript of the book "Interlinking of Indian Rivers" written by Shri Radha Kant Bharati. The book discusses several aspects of interlinking of Indian Rivers in an interesting background of available data, information, studies and analysis of water resources of the country and prevailing water management practices covering conservation and quality aspects as well. The Author has made use of his academic background, editorial experience and his association with leading organizations in the sector in incorporating and analyzing critical views of scholars, eminent engineers and concerned institutions.

All the chapters of the book are well conceived and neatly placed and summarizes crucial aspects of generated thoughts and blueprints of interlinking of Indian rivers which need to be considered fiy Planners and Policy Makers.

I am sure this Book will be appreciated by general readers, students, academicians and all having interest in the area of water resources, management and planning.

A.B. Pandya
Chairman,
Central Water Commission
New Delhi

A great engineer and Minister of Irrigation & Power Dr. K.L. Rao had indicated several points regarding Water Resources in his book Water Wealth of India—

"...Water resources development involves not only comprehensive planning from engineering angles but must also consider the economic, legal and social aspects......"

"...India will be forced to face many difficult water problems earlier than many other countries, because it has a huge population base and numbers are increasing rapidly year after year....."

"...It is erroneously considered that India has vast water resources...... "

"...The needs for water are growing in various fields. The precious waters of India have, therefore, to be exploited quickly and wisely and at the sametime protected against pollution and wasteful uses......"

Interlinking of Rivers

Contents

Swept Away by the four Rivers

Once a guru was giving a discourse; thousands of his followers gathered to listen to him. God sent his messenger to check who would all be interested to 1 come out of samsara or worldly life to be present permanently in heaven, in nirvana. The messenger went around asking people but none seemed ready. Finally, an 80-year-old man showed some interest and agreed to go with the messenger after he finished what he intended to do. The man asked for time to get his grandchildren married.

When the messenger returned to take him to the heaven, he found that old man had died and taken rebirth as a dog in the same household. As a dog he wanted to safeguard his children's property. When the mess-enger returned after some years, he found that dog had died and was reborn as. a frog near the kitchen drain of the family. The god's messenger dutifully reminded the frog of his old promise, the frog decisively said he was happy as he got surplus food and drink from the drain. So it is that heaven became last priority.

In the uddhist Abhidharm scriptures say that being swept away by the strong current of four big inner rivers desire, samsaric existence, views and ignorance.

When we see a beautiful human or object, we go beyondjust appreciating the beauty by getting attached to it and wanting to take possession. We are unable to take our eyes and mind off it. Likewise, we create many imaginary things which are not there in reality like name, fame, position and glory. We develop and nurture such imaginary ideas and do not let go of them. Sometimes the glories may have already been achieved, then we are anxious of losing what is achieved. Our insecurity makes us build strong forces to protect our glory from all that we see as challenges or threats to it. And so we flow with the

River of views, river of desire is that which carruies one to illusive states of mind such as viewing are the body as "I", having extreme views on any subject, regarding one's own point of view, moral codes and rituals as being supreme. This extends to one's own race, language, tradition and so on as being; supreme: This view eventually leads chauvinism and fanaticism, and could lead to violence including errorist: activity.

River of ignorance is the cause of all troubles ignorance is not bliss; because it implies holding on to the very opposite of the fundamental truth. Hence, it is the mother of all troubles.

River of samsaric existence is focussed inwards rather than deriving from the external sense objects. There is no desire, no sleep, no worry, no emotional suffering and no regrets. One remains for very long in the blissful experience of samadhi. But it is still linked to samsaric existence. However, a time comes when the strength of samadhi is exhausted; and one gets caught in cyclic existence.

On the whole, in the samsaric situation, nothing is really desirable and dependable. With this notion, one should try to free one self from the samsaric situation instead of clinging on to something or other that holds; us down in these rivers. Like the old man in the story.

L.P. Lama

Preface

Transfer of surplus waters to the deficit areas and thereby improving the economy and quality of life equitably across the country has been a dream of the people of India since long. Such transfers have of late, been named as Interlinking of Rivers (ILR) programme.

After independence, considerable thought and planning effort has been devoted to the scheme. Dr. K.L. Rao's, Ganga Cauvery link and Captain Dastur's garland canal proposals have captured the imagination of the people across the country and cutting across ages and generations as well as backgrounds, perhaps every knowledgeable citizen of the country is aware of such proposals and benefits that can accrue from them.

Government of India prepared a National Perspective Plan in 1980, which identified Inter basin transfers that can be implemented in Peninsular India and also transfers from Himalayan Rivers of Ganga and Brahmputra Basin Rivers. The national perspective plan has undergone further firming up through National Water Development Agency a society constituted under Ministry of Water Resources with states as members. Systematic efforts to study and plan the transfers have been in operation since 1982.

The issue needing the inter basin transfers have been flagged since long, the non-implementation of the same on a nationwide scale even after a lapse of about 30 years since the inception of the idea is puzzling many. There are several types of opinions expressed by various sources favouring and arguing against the programme. Biggest need is to generate a consensus amongst various stakeholders to facilitate the implementation of the programme. Perhaps, now is the time to sift through the opinions and examine the same in a dispassionate manner.

The Supreme Court order asking the government to implement the inter-linking of rivers project is expected to change the water situation. Former Minister Suresh Prabhu, who headed the task force on this project during the NDA rule, explains the necessity of the project and said "I welcome the order. I am of the view that inter-linking of rivers is not a panacea to all issues faced by India but the ideas thrown up by the task force, chaired by me, in the report need to bre pondered over seriously. Water is something that cannot be created by man; it cannot be manufactured in any factory or cannot be imported on a scale like oil, which is meeting 80 per cent of our demand. Therefore, management of the available water resources within our sovereign geographical boundaries is necessary to cater to the requirement of the growing population and the changing life style. I have been arguing time and again that politics should not be involved in crucial issues, including water. I have been quite consistent on my stand. In fact, I strongly believe there is a need for a political consensus on such issues to address the national challenges.–"

In this context the book provides a platform to water resources policy makers, professionals to come together and share ideas and experiences and challenges relating to implementation of the project.

I am thankful to Mr. A.J. Sehgal of Lotus Press for accepting to publish the work.

–Radha Kant Bharati

56, Nagin Lake
Peera Garhi
New Delhi-110087

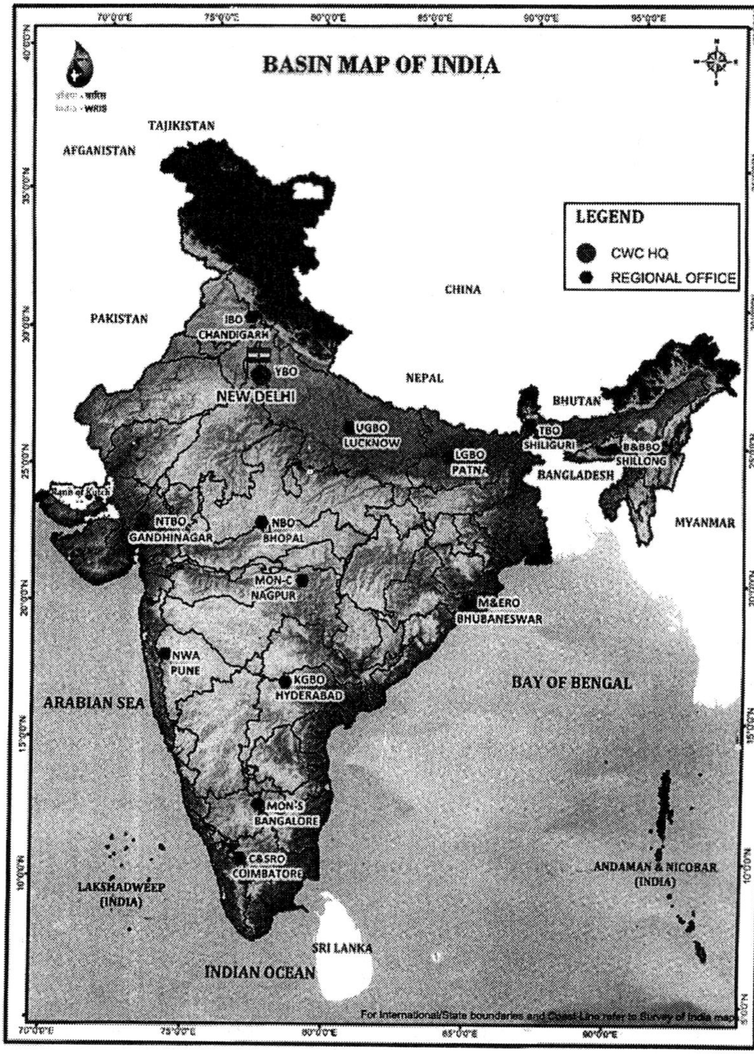

Courtsey (Govt. of India)

Chapter 1

Rivers of Indian Sub-Continent

It is mentioned in the Indian Puranic literature:

> "Rivers are like mother for the country and mountains like the father. This father is a magnanimous thoughtful resolute archaic man and the rivers are conscious liberators, swift and source of knowledge, when clouds which roam free in the open sky spend themselves at the bedstead of the horizon after creating a commotion, then Mother Earth conceives that life giving man with the halo through its rivers in arteries. These water-filled streams fill the earth with the power of procreation and energy. It is these streams flowing on the landmass which act as the blood-pumping arteries in the body." (*Kalidasa in Raghuvansham*)

In our India, the land of many rivers, the role of river streams has since long been as important one. Consequently, various efforts have been made for harnessing the river waters, proof of which is still visible at many places in North and South India. The *Raja ki Nahar* at Palampur in Himachal Pradesh, *Fakir ki Panchakki* in Aurangabad (Maharashtra) and the Cauvery river dam at Tanjour in Tamil Nadu are a few such examples.

After independence India had to initially face many types of problems among which poverty, unemployment drought, floods and backwardness have been the major ones. But the world's biggest democracy, India with patience, took steps to solve these problems by planned development. As a result, reservoirs were constructed after building huge dams on the rivers. Industries too gained the necessary impetus due to the irrigation of fields and generation of hydroelectricity. The Green Revolution that occurred in the 70s (1971-81) made the country self-sufficient in food production. Behind its success too, was the important role played by the proper harnessing of water resources at the national level.

For the sake of convenience, the rivers of India have been divided into two categories:–

On the basis of origin–

1. Himalayan rivers–
2. Peninsular rivers–

On the basis of their courses–

1. Those which flow into the Bay of Bengal–
2. Those which flow into the Arabian Sea–

Many geologist and specialists have suggested that the Indian rivers be studied after dividing them in the following three groups:–

1. The Ganga-Indus-Brahamaputra rivers in North India
2. The plateau rivers in South India, and
3. Those rivers which do not belong to either category.

Among the Indian rivers, the Ganga is regarded as the foremost. The Ganga is not just an ordinary river, but a living symbol of holistic Indianness. From the earliest times, it has been mother 'Ganga' for all the inhabitants of this country. From the ancient to the modern period, many poets and writers have sung paeans of its glory. The stream that flows from the Gomukh cave in the Gangotri glacier situated in the mighty Himalayas is called Alakhnanda till Dev Prayag and turns Mandakini in Rudra Prayag. Descending from the slopes of the mighty Himalaya, the Bhagirathi enters the plains at *Har-ki-Pauri* in Haridwar. The Ganga, in the plains ahead, flows towards the east, then turning south-east, reaches West Bengal. Bearing the name of Hooghly, the Ganga gets divided into many streams here. In the end, forming a huge delta at Sundarbans along with the streams of Brahmaputra, it flows into the Bay of Bengal.

Among the tributaries of this major river are the Yamuna, Sonebhadra, Ramganga, Gomati, Saryu, Gandak and Kosi. Watered by the Ganga, the State, of Uttar Pradesh and Uttarakhand have seen many famous towns coming up in its green plains. Among them, Haridwar, Kanpur, Allahabad and Varanasi are worth mentioning. Flowing east, the Ganga enters Bihar through Ghazipur and Mughalsarai. Flowing past Buxar and Chausa, it reaches Bhojpur and the capital Patna. From there, flowing between the hogious of Mithila and Magadh, the Ganga crosses the Farakka Barrage and enters West Bengal. From, here, the main stream flows south.

The city of Kolkata is situated on the banks of this branch called Hooghly.

The origin of Brahamaputra, a major river of North-Eastern India is near the Mansarovar Lake in Tibet. Due to the enormity of its flow and because of mythology, Brahmaputra is called a great river. Initially, this stream flows towards the east in the Tibet region. Then it turns south-west with hair pin bend and travelling through the Himalayan ranges flows into India forming a deep valley. Fed by the waters of its tributaries like Lohit, Dibang and the Teesta, the Brahamaputra becomes even mightier. The Brahamaputra valley which extends from the north-eastern region to Assam, is considered important from the geographical, political and strategic points of view. Flowing west in Assam, the course of the river Brahamaputra turns south and enters Bangladesh. It then gets divided into many streams and after mixing with the water of the river Ganga, forms the muddy delta of Sunderban and then flows into the Bay of Bengal.

The origin of the river Indus which forms the border of many countries is also near Mansarovar in Tibet. Flowing west from its point of origin, the Indus stream forms a deep valley cutting across the Karakoram ranges in the western Himalayas and crossing the extreme northern part of India, turn south from Attock in the Hindukush mountains. Flowing past the ancient sites of the Indus Valley Civilization, this river flows into the Arabian Sea near Karachi after having crossed the Sindh province. In North India, there are many rivers which flow down from the lofty snow-clad peaks of the Himalayas. Of these, Jhelum is famous for the *shikaras* floating on the Dal Lake. In Himachal Pradesh, Chandrabhaga, formed by the union of Chandra and Bhaga is the gift of the Chamba Valley in the Dhauladhar ranges. The Ravi, Beas and the Sutlej too flow from this region, and flowing west-south, meet the river Indus.

The Vindhyachal range of mountains criss-crosses the central part of India. From the traditional and geological point of view, it is regarded as the dividing line between North and South India or as its meeting point. From the highlands of this plateau area, flow many streams. The plateau of Amarkantak is the origin of both Sonebhadra and the Narmada. These rivers are streams which flow in Tuft opposite directions. The turbulent Narmada originates from Amarkantak and sliding over the marble rocks at Bheraghat flows west and enters the Gulf of Cambay, near Bharuch while the Sonebhadra forming a quiet and massive stream flows in a north-east directions and meets the Ganga in Central Bihar. Besides these rivers, others like the Chambal, Betwa Tons and several other small streams originate in Madhya Pradesh and Chatis Garh.

Among the rivers of South India, the Cauvery is regarded as holy and munificient as the Ganga in North India. Originating from the plateau of Coorg at Tal Kaveri this river flows in an eastern and then in a southern direction. Flowing past Karnataka through the middle of Tamil Nadu, the Cauvery drains its water into the Bay of Bengal. The holy river Cauvery is famous not only for the temples and ghats on its banks but also for dams, like the Krishna Sagar and the canals of Thanjavur. One river which provides water in abundance to those living along its course is the river Krishna. Originating from the Mahabaleshwar hills in Maharashtra, the river Krishna flows through the entire stretch of Andhra Pradesh and drains into the Bay of Bengal. Tungabhadra and Malprabha are its main tributaries. The river originating from the Triyambak Hills near Nasik is Godavari. It is known as the Ganga of the South and flows east through Maharashtra and Andhra Pradesh and drains its waters into the Bay of Bengal.

Originating near andakaranya in Central India and flowing in a south-east direction, the Mahanadi crossing the borders of Madhya Pradesh enters Orissa where under the Hirakud Project, a big dam, a reservoir and a power station have been constructed.

It is worth mentioning that in many regions of India, besides these major rivers, there are several other rivers of various descriptions. The river Chambal, famous for the Gandhi Sagar Dam, originates from Madhya Pradesh and flowing east-south from the borders of Madhya Pradesh, Rajasthan and in Uttar Pradesh, it flows into the river Yamuna.

Similarly, there are rivers like the Damodar, Gandak, Kosi, Suvarna Rekha, Tawa and Teesta, on which many dams have been built under multipurpose projects. The Tamraparni, Kshipra, Rihand and the Ragit rivers are mentionable in this regard.

In a country like India, with a monsoon and tropical type of climate, it is a universal fact that its rivers are not just dying streams but are instead part of its folk culture, full of life and emotions like the female lead characters. One gets the proof of this spontaneously in the Indian society and families. For example, in the past and even now, families in the different regions of India name their daughters after the rivers like Ganga, Padma, Cauvery, Gomati, Kshipra, Godavari, Krishna etc.

The another interesting fact about these rivers which symbolizes the Indian culture is that not only rivers like the Ganga and the Yamuna, but almost all others too have mythological or puranic legends associated with them in which the streams are described as having a human form. While bathing and during the inauguration ceremonies, the names of five major rivers are invoked through recitation of hymns, for the sake of glory and prestige of water–

गंगे च यमुने चैव, गोदावरी सरस्वती।
नर्मदे सिंधु कावेरी, जलेअस्मिन सन्निधं कुरु।।

●●●

Chapter 2

Role of Irrigation

Various analyses of the role of irrigation in India's agriculture have shown that irrigation has played a core role in agricultural production and growth. Although gross irrigated area (currently about 90 million ha includes double cropping) is about one third of total cropped area in India; the production from irrigated lands greatly exceeds the productivity of rain fed farming. In a monsoon dependent farming system with rains unreliable and large areas with rainfall less than 1,000 mm per annum, irrigation has been a crucial input for agricultural production. Irrigation enables a higher productive potential from the lands and significant production response from associated use of high yielding varieties, fertilizer and other inputs. At the national and regional levels, agricultural growth and rural development have closely followed the growth and regional pattern of irrigation expansion. The production impact of Indian irrigation has occurred through four routes; cultivated area expansion, cropping pattern shifts, productivity enhancement and increase in reliability. Ascertaining irrigation's precise contribution is however difficult. This is in part because there are no official Indian statistical data summaries giving the break down of agricultural production under irrigated or rain fed conditions. Nevertheless, various estimates point to a contribution from irrigated agriculture to overall agricultural production of about two thirds and under some estimates an even higher contribution. Even more difficult is the assessment of irrigated agriculture's contribution to agricultural growth. It is probable, however, that irrigated agriculture has contributed the bulk of past agricultural growth. Today, the average aggregate productivity of irrigated agriculture per unit of land would seem to be seven times than a rainfed agriculture. While estimates of impact of irrigation vary, all point to its significance in Indian agriculture and its importance to past agricultural growth.

With nearly all arable land now under cultivation and limited progress to date with major technological breakthroughs for rainfed crops, irrigated agriculture will likely remain the key contributor to India's agricultural development. It is clearly of far reaching importance to enhance productivity from rainfed agriculture. Although probably contributing less than one third of India's agricultural production and likely still a marginal contributor to agricultural growth, rainfed agriculture occupies two thirds of India's cropped area and for most rural communities is still the primary source of livelihood. In terms of the relative share in India'screated irrigation potential, surface water in canals accounts for 39%. Ground water (with a major private sector involvement) for 47% and other water source for 14%. Over the 1951 to 1955 period, the publicly created and managed major and medium schemes increased threefold while the privately created and managed groundwater segment increased sevenfold. Regionally, the major states in terms of irrigation area are Uttar Pradesh, Andhra Pradesh, Madhya Pradesh, Chattis Garh, Punjab, Rajasthan, Bihar, Haryana, Gujarat, Tamilnadu, Karnataka, Maharashtra, Orissa and West Bengal. In most states, groundwater irrigated area exceeds the surface irrigated area.

Most important contribution of irrigation to Indian agriculture was in facilitating the spread of the Green revolution. The expansion of irrigation from the mid-1960's period the enabling environment for use of the new high yielding varieties and fertilizer, pushing the production frontier to a new height and transforming the rural sector. The major gainers in terms of both productivity and area share were wheat and rice. As a result, food-grain production increased from 51 million tons (mt) in 1951 to 199 mt by 1997 and a compound annual growth rate of 3.0%. now 25 mt. The average food grain yields nationwide increased from 1.0 tons/ha to 1.5 tons/ha. Irrigation expansion has also imparted a greater degree of stability to farm production. In contrast to the chronic spectre and actualities of famines in India during the 1950s and 1960s, the country has been by the large self- sufficient in food-grains since the early 2004 and in the last decade India has become a net grain exporter. India has now become the world's largest producer of milk and cashew nuts second largest producers of rice, wheat, sugarcane, groundnut and vegetables, third largest producer of wheat, cotton, sorghum, potatoes, coffee, rapeseed-mustard and the sixth largest producer of maize. Irrigation is a major factor that made this possible.

National Commission for Integrated Water Resources Development Plan (NCIWRDP) has estimated that increase in irrigation facilities alone has contributed to about 52% increase in food grains production and improved management, agricultural practices and high yielding varieties have contributed to 48% increase in food-grains production. Once water is available, crop lands begin to produce more and become less prone to droughts. Slowly, over time, animal based production also increases thus raising nutrition and health levels of the people.

With an estimated two-thirds or more of agricultural production from irrigated agriculture, employment impact is clearly significant. The incremental employment generated by the irrigation potential created during the Eighth Plan has been estimated by Government at 8.7 million person-years. Since irrigation development forges inter-sectoral and initerregional linkages through output growth and income flow, its employment and income impacts have powerful multiplier effects. A 100 rupee worth of irrigation induced incremental agricultural output is estimated to generate Rs. 105 worth of additional output in manufacturing and Rs. 114 in the tertiary service sector, employing an overall non-farm output multiplier of 2.19. Irrigation has also played a role in poverty alleviation. Between 1964 and 1994, the national average prices of rice and wheat, the major Indian food staples, declined by 2.2% and 3.3% per annum in real terms, respectively. A significant inverse relation between the incidence of poverty and the extent of irrigation development has been found in several cross-sectional studies based on both districts and agro climatic sub-zones. While incidence of poverty is as high as 69% in districts with less than 10% of cropped area under irrigation, it is about 26% in districts where irrigation covers more than 50% area and just 10% in Punjab and Haryana with over 70% of their cropped area under irrigation. Interlinking of rivers was an ambitious plan of the Atal Behari Vajpayee's government and it has gained new saliency following the dangerous precedent set by the Amarinder Singh government in the SYL crisis. Vajpayee's letter to Prime Minister Manmohan Singh on Monday, urging him to convene an all-party meeting to evolve a consensus on sharing of river waters, not only indicates the urgent need to solve the water crisis but is a welcome break in the NDA-UPA government standoff over the past few years. The letter is reproduced below–

Dear Prime Minister,

It is a matter of grave concern that the sharing of river waters, which is a national issue, is turning into rivalry between states driven by populist gains.

I am worried that a conflagration could consume our country. Water is an essential commodity, which arouses the deepest emotions among people, particularly our farmers. Oil is called the liquid gold of the modern age; water is the true liquid gold now. Some people say that in twenty years' time, wars will be fought in the world over water not oil. In our country, we have always considered water holy, pavitra; we worship our rivers because they give us life. I believe that it is our duty to use our vision to make water into a factor that unites our country. We know that when water begins to divide us, it becomes an acid that tears apart brothers. It was this concern that made us dream of a system by which the water basins of our country could be coordinated for the mutual benefit of everyone, so that water could be prevented from being wasted into the ocean. Some useful work was done by the Task Force headed by Shri Suresh Prabhu. The Task Force did create widespread awareness on the urgent need of water resources management in the country and the important of interlinking of rivers as a means of a comprehensive approach to solve the problem. Unfortunately your government has wound it up at a time when emotions on the issue of water have risen alarmingly.

Everyone has a viewpoint on the sharing of river waters. Punjab has its needs; so do Haryana and Rajasthan. Every state, every political party has a right to take a stand in a democracy. That is not the issue. However, a democracy only functions by mutual consent, not by arbitrary action. Passions are building that need to be calmed immediately, before they burst into flames. I urge that all of us treat this as a national problem that cold degenerate into a crisis, and seek amicable answers to dangerous questions. For this purpose I suggest that you urgently convene a meeting of the leaders of all political parties to evolve a consensual approach to sharing of rivers waters.

Since the issue covered in this letter vitally affects the fate of our country, I propose to release it to the media after it is delivered to your office.

With warm regards,

Yours sincerely,

Sd/-

(A. B. Vajpayee)

View of Indira Gandhi Canal the Result of Interlinking of Rivers

Water of Hope

Water-flow form River to Canal

Harnessing Water Power
Dehar Power Plant on river Sutlaj

Chapter 3

River Water Conservation and Quality

Improved water management on field and improved agricultural techniques could surely increase yields of both rain fed and irrigated agriculture. This has been happening all through the past 30 years or so. However, there is some evidence of plateauing in regard to rice and wheat in the high productivity pockets. Also while better yields can more easily be obtained on an experimental plot in controlled condition or even in the field of an individual progressive farmer improving averages over a region is an extremely slow and painful process. Even while concentrating on the process, it may perhaps be better to make reasonable assumptions about the growth of productivity. In general, management changes which are based on human resource development including changes in skills knowledge and attitude are slow to pick-up and either large or fast changes cannot be expected under these corcumstances.

Much has been said about the wasteful use in irrigation and in particular about the low efficiencies in distribution and field applications of irrigation from surface sources. Typically, in a large surface canal system, out of 100 units of water diverted from the river upto 45 units could be lost as seepage in the distribution network, upto 10 units could be lost through over irrigation in the field and only 35 units may serve the desired purpose of increased evapo-transipitation through irrigated crops. Considering these, it is argued that water saving is the easiest method of increasing the resource base. This however, is not always true. What is loss for the surface irrigation system is often an important gain from the ground water sub-system. In many parts of India particularly in north Rajasthan, Punjab, Haryana and Uttar Pradesh much of the large scale ground water development is based on mopping up of these additional resource available from surface irrigation. Thus, from an overall basin consideration, the system can be quite efficient even though the surface distribution system is inefficient. On these considerations, the International Water Management Institute (IWMI), Srilanka has advocated the use of basin efficiency concept. Mechanised irrigation application such as drips and sprinklers also save some water. These allow small and frequent irrigation and thus the loss due to over irrigation through large doses as is common in the conventional system could be saved. This could be around 10% of the diverted water. In addition, drips on tree crops save evaporation from soils since the soils trip in between two rows of trees is not wetted. However, these require additional capital costs and additional infrastructure through storages, filters, pumps etc., and this becomes practicable only in few horticultural crops to fetch a good price.

Domestic and industrial requirements are comparatively smaller in quantity, but this water is costlier because of the treatment. Domestic systems can have upto 30% "unaccounted water", part of it due to leakages from pipes and remaining due to pilferage. The pilfered water merely represents a financial loss although the social purpose may have been met. Leakage control is an important measure, more for saving costly water than for saving the quantity of water. While such measures are necessary and a good management tools, they are unlikely to meet the large increasing needs of water in future. Reuse and recycling constitutes a very important measure of stretching the limited water resources. Often the effluent from domestic use after treatment can be effectively used for irrigation. This can allow the use of residual nutrients by the crop, and in the process the river waters would not get polluted. For industrial waters also, treatment and recovery of pollutants allows the natural waters to be of a reasonably good quality so that these could be used on the downstream. However, in general in the water short regions of India, most returned water whether treated or not gets used in agriculture. Thus, while treatment is essential, in quantitative terms the stretching of the resources is already taking place. The control of population to reduce demands is of course desirable but in view of the efforts already being made this could hardly be considered as an alternative for inter-basin transfers. Reasonably effective population control programme needs of farm the basis of population projections which go into the planning of inter-basin transfers. The much larger issue of population control needs to be tackled as a national campaign, but need not be linked to the issue of inter-basin transfers.

Changing of human settlement patterns to suit water availability has been occurring naturally in the history, but even then the water deficient areas of India already have population densities beyond what could be sustained by the available resources. However, the social stresses involved in artificial change in settlement patterns would perhaps preclude the use of such measures as an alternative to water transfers. While management measures concentrating on demand management are necessary, augmenting supplies also appears essential. Proposals for inter-basin transfer need to be viewed in this context.

Environmental Impacts of Inter-basin Transfers

The Planners are familiar with the social and environmental concerns caused by small, medium and large in-basin projects. Over years, the awareness about such concerns and the methods for dealing with the adverse impacts caused by such concerns have changed considerably and an acceptable methodology of evaluating and meeting the concern through legal policy related and management measures has evolved more or less in a satisfactory manner.

Several contradictory views have been expressed that inter-basin transfers may cause socioeconomic and environmental impacts much different from those caused by in-basin developments. These differences could be both due to the large size of the project and due to the different nature of the project which involves long distance water transfers through large and long canals. For example, the large storages and long links could involve a much larger resettlement problem than the nation is used to. The link canals may involve large scale interruption of natural drainage system and also a large barrier between neighbouring communities. These are the problems created by the size. But, the very nature of inter-basin transfers could also lead to inadvertent introduction of flora and fauna alien to the recipient basin from the donar basin. This introduced flora and fauna could theoretically grow to a proportion where it becomes a menace to the ecology of the recipient area and can disturb the ecological balances.

Impacts Assessment for Inter-basin Transfers

The social and environmental concerns associated with these interbasin transfers would mainly on account of the largeness of the totality of the measures in the region in which the system of links passes. Each individual storage dam such as the Ichampally, the Polavaram, the Manibhadra/ Tikarapara etc. involved in the peninsular links would not be much different in its storage or in its displacement from the large reservoirs like Gandhisagar, Sardar Sarovar, Srisailam, Nagarjunasagar etc. which are existing. Similarly, we already have experienced about large canals exceeding discharge capacities of 1000 m^3/sec and the link canals would be not of much larger magnitude though these would be of much larger links. The issue of inadvertent introduction of alien flora and fauna is important since it could cause a very serious ecological problem. While this needs a detailed study, preliminary verbal enquiries have not brought out any such possibilities. The existing inter-basin transfers in India do not seem to have experienced any such problem. Perhaps the ecology of the various regions of India are not dissimilar. The Himalayan regions with their tundras and tagas could perhaps have a markedly different ecology and transfer of waters of these regions to the peninsula may require a more detail study of these aspects.

In this context, National River Conservation Plan can be taken into consideration.

National River Conservation Plan

Cleaning of a river is a mammoth task requiring the involvement of all the stakeholders, in the project, viz, Central Government, State Government, Local Bodies, Implementing Agencies, NGOs, General Public, Users, etc. Also, Cleaning of pollution is not a one-time effort and the demands of river cleaning go on increasing with the increase in the population and expansion of townships and the success of the scheme depends on continuous efforts to be made by all these agencies. The objective of the River Action Plan is to improve the water quality of the major rivers, which are the major fresh water source in the country through the implementation of pollution abatement schemes.

The important works taken up under the NRCP include

1. Interception and diversion works to capture the raw sewage flowing into the river through drains and their diversion for treatment.

2. Provision of Sewage Treatment Plant for treating the diverted sewage.
3. Provision of Low Cost Sanitation works to prevent open defecation on river banks.
4. Provision of Electric Crematoria and Improved Wood Creamatoria to conserve the use of wood and help in reducing river water pollution and ensuring proper creamation of bodies brought to the burning ghats.
5. River front development works such as improvement of bathing ghats etc.
6. Other minor miscellaneous works like plantation, public awareness etc.

Ganga Action Plan Phase I

GAP Phase I was the first attempt by the Government of India to clean the river Ganga. The plan was formulated on the basis of a comprehensive survey of the Ganga basin carried out by the CPCB in 1984. The survey indicated that out of total measurable point sources of pollution, 75% was on account of municipal sewage from towns located along the banks of the river and the remaining 25% was on account of industrial effluents. At the time of launching, the main objective of GAP Phase I was to improve the water quality of Ganga to acceptable standards by preventing the pollution load reaching the river. But the result is not encouraging.

Rivers Covered Under NRCP

The rivers covered under NRCP are:

Adyar	Ganga	Musi	Tunga
Betwa	Godawari	Narmada	Tungabhadra
Bhadra	Gomti	Penniar	Tambraparani

Brahmini	Khan	Pamba	Vennar
Cauvery	Krishna	Sabarmati	Vagai
Cooum	Kshipra	Satluj	Wainganga
Chambal	Mahanadi	Subernarekha	Yamuna
Damodar	Mandovi	Tapti	

Progress Made

859 projects with a value of Rs. 3253.92 crore have been sanctioned under NRCP. This is in addition to 261 projects sanctioned under GAP Phase I. The total expenditure incurred till 31.6.2004 under NRCP is Rs. 1645.37 crore, including the State's share. A Sewage Treatment capacity of 1045 mld had been created under this plan so far.

Water Quality

The Water Quality Monitoring of the Ganga river done at selected locations revealed that the river water quality has shown improvement over the pre-GAP period water quality. It has been observed that in 1986, the bio-chemical oxygen demand (BOD) which is an indicator of pollution of river water quality was ranging from 5.5 to 15.5 mg/l in the critical stretch of Ganga from Kannuaj to Varanasi. As against this, the values of BOD in 2003 in the stretch of Kannauj to Kanpur and Allahabad to Varanasi is (1.20-6.1 mg/l) and (2.50-5.4 mg/l) respectively. The values of BOD at Allahabad upstream has been as 8.00 mg/l. Similarly, Dissolved Oxygen (DO) levels which indicate health of the river, were in the range of 5.9 to 6.6 mg/l in 1986 in the Allahabad-Varanasi stretch and in 2003 the range improved to 7.2 to 8.10 mg/l.

Progress during Tenth Five Year Plan

An outlay of Rs. 1417 crore and Rs. 220 crore have been provided under NRCP and NLCP during Tenth Five Year

Plan out of which Rs. 816.55 and Rs. 62.19 crore are expected to be spent under these Plans by the end of the these financial year (2004-05).

Further the National Environment Policy-2004 formulated by Ministry of Environment and Forests is an appreciable land mark in this direction.

Inter-Linking Rivers is the most ambitious project in Indian history, much more challenging than the Prime Minister's Golden Quadrilateral and North-South, East-West corridors.

Since the days of the great poet Subramanyam Bharati, who dreamt of linking the Ganga and Cauveri, stalwarts have been thinking, discussing, programming and presenting voluminous reports on this grand dream.

Decades ago, Union Minister for Irrigation and Power Dr. K.L. Rao and later Captain Dastoor mooted the idea of garland canals inter-linking rivers. The unstinted support to the inter-basin water transfer links by President APJ Abdul Kalam and the then Prime Minister Atal Bihari Vajpayee, within a few years, signifies the project's importance.

The network of waterways would bring down transportation costs. The project would create crores of construction-jobs, especially for unskilled and semi-skilled rural workers, and new job opportunities in manufacturing, transportation, agriculture, fisheries and tourism sectors. The urbanization trend can be reversed by creating farm and off-farm jobs in rural areas through the project.

Intangible benefits include inculcating the sense and spirit of national unity. By bringing technology to the rural areas, the urban-rural divide will becomes less intense. The Green Revolution in hitherto water-starved areas will bring down the menace of naxalism in Bihar, Jharkhand, Orissa Chattishgarh and West Bengal, a major reason for which is the lack of jobs, and improve national security.

It is well-known fact that India is blessed with good water resources in the form of rivers spanning 170 thousand km, water bodies over 68 million hectares and vast ground water resources. The annual utilization potential of surface water is estimated to be 690 billion cubic metres and the same for ground water is 432 billion cubic metres.

But much of this river water is wasted by flowing into the sea. While large part of Northern and Eastern India suffers from terrible floods every year; yet the other part of India continues suffering from drought. If India has to prosper, inter-linking the rivers is the most imperative.

We need to find a way to transfer water from surplus basins to deficit basins and this is what the Government is embarking upon. It is nobody's case that there are no pitfalls and problems, rather there are plenty of them. Anyone can imagine what types of difficulties successive Governments faced in constructing the Sardar Sarovar Dam. Ultimately, Supreme Court had to silence the agitation. Today millions are reaping the benefits of the dam. Bhakhra Nangal Dam too was questioned, but today its water is flowing up to Barmer and Jaisalmer in Rajasthan. This mega project addresses the problem of water resources in totality. The question of resources of about Rs. 7 lakh crore is also raised. Where would it come from? About 30 lakh people may even be displaced. Contrary to popular notion, migration and displacement ultimately results in economic betterment of the groups and societies who suffer the transition. Rivers are a very sensitive issue with local people as well as the States. We have witnessed the Cauveri dispute, a prickly problems in the relations between Karnataka and Tamil Nadu. Among the northern states, Punjab, Haryana and Rajasthan too are entangled in similar tensions. But these examples should not act as a deterrent for this mega project. Ecological and environmental issues are also raised, though not without basis. But quite often they are highly exaggerated. Eventually the project would address the problem of water scarcity wholesomely.

With the beginning of the 21st century India has gathered the courage to solve the problem of water scarcity and turbulent floods just within two decades.

●●●

Chapter 4

Need for Interlinking

The rainfall over the subcontinent fo India is primarily orographic, associated with tropical depressions originating in the Arabian Sea and the Bay of Bengal. The summer monsoon accounts for more than 85 per cent of the precipitation in the Indian Sub-continent. The uncertainty of occurrence of rainfall marked by prolonged dry spells and fluctuations in seasonal and annual rainfall is a serious problem for the country. Large parts of the Haryana, Maharashtra, Andhra Pradesh, Rajasthan, Gujarat, Madhya Pradesh , Karnataka and Tamil Nadu are not only deficient in rainfall but also subject to large variations, resulting in frequent draught and causing immense hardship to the population and enormous loss to the nation. The water availability even for drinking purposes becomes critical, particularly in the eaily summer months as the rivers dry up and the ground water recedes. Regional variations in the rainfall lead to situations when some parts of the country do not have enough water even for raising a single crop. On the other hand excess rainfall occurring in some parts of the country create havoc due to floods.

Irrigation using river water and ground water has been the prime factor for raising the food grain production in our country from a mere 50 million tons in the 1950s to more than 200 million tons at present, leading us to attain self-sufficiency in food. Irrigated area has increased from 22 million hectares to 95 million hectares during this period. The population of India, which is more than 1000 million at present, is expected to increase to 1500 to 1800 million in the year 2050 and that would require about 450 million tons of food grains. With the consumption level most likely to increase in the future we may have to plan for a production level of at least 500 million tons. For meeting this requirement, it would be necessary to increase irrigation potential to 160 million hectares for all crops by 2050. India's maximum irrigation potential that could be created through conventional sources has been assessed to be about 140 million hectares. For attaining a potential of 160 million hectares, other strategies shall have to be evolved.

In several states of India floods are a recurring feature particularly in the Brahamaputra and Ganga rivers in which almost 60% of the river flows of our country occur. Flood damages which were Rs. 52 crore in 1953 have gone upto Rs. 5,846 crore in 1998 with annual average being Rs. 1,343 crore, affecting the states of Assam, Bihar, West Bengal and Uttar Pradesh along with untold human suffering. On the other hand large areas in the states of Rajasthan, Gujarat, Andhra Pradesh, Karnataka and Tamil Nadu face recurring droughts. As much as 85% of drought prone area falls in these states.

One of the most effective ways to increase the irrigation potential for increasing the food grain production, mitigate floods and droughts and reduce regional imbalance in the availability of water is the interlinking of our rivers to transfer water from the surplus rivers to deficit areas. The Brahamaputra and the Ganga–particularly their northern tributarien, Deccan area Mahanadi, Godavari and west flowing rivers originating from the Western Ghats are found to be surplus in water resources. If we can build storage reservoirs on these rivers and connect them to other parts of the country, regional imbalances could be reduced significantly and lot of benefits by way of additional irrigation, domestic and industrial water supply, hydro-power generation, navigational facilities, etc. would accrue.

The discussion on the concept of inter-basin transfer of water started long back about 65 years ago, on the initiative of Dr. K.L. Rao, former Union Minister of Irrigation and Power in preparing proposals for National Water Grid, followed by Garland Canal, through Capt. Dastur's Concept. After several years Government of India had set up an organization called National Water Development Agency (NWDA) in 1982 which has in the last 32 years done extensive studies of the various possible links for inter-basin water transfers.

Though the concept is rational and can solve a lot of problems. But it has also thrown open several delicate issues– the constitutional provisions, the existing legal provisions, water ownership, political support, willingness of participating states etc. Various proposals involving inter-basin transfers within India on a large scale have been and are being studied for about last 50 years. In the 1970's, Dr. K. L. Rao, prepared proposals for the National Water Grid. His proposal better known as the Ganga Kaveri Link consisted of 1640 km link from Ganga near Patna to transfer the Ganga waters during high flow to the south. The proposal also envisaged the Brahamaputra Ganga Link and Western Link. Another proposal which received considerable publicity was that of Captain Dastur. This proposal better known as the Garland Canal consisted of a 4200 km long Himalayan Canal, a 9300 km long Southern Garland Canal and a connection between the two systems through pipelines near Delhi and Patna. After intensive study of these proposals, the Ministry of Irrigation and the Central Water Commission in 1980, prepared a National Perspective Plan comprising of two components namely (*i*) The Himalayan River Component and (*ii*) The Peninsula River Component. The outline of the National

Perspective Plan was widely discussed at political level and a decision was taken by the then Prime Minister Smt. Indira Gandhi to start immediately.

National Perspective Plan for Water Resources Development

The continued interest shown by many people gave impetus to study interbasin water transfer proposals. The then Ministry of Irrigation (now Ministry of Water Resources) and CWC formulated a National Perspective Plan (NPP) for Water Resources Development in 1980 envisaging interbasin transfer of water from surplus basins to deficit basins/areas with a view to minimize the regional imbalances and optimally utilize the available water resources.

The broad approach adopted in the NPP is that; existing uses have been kept undisturbed, it is within the framework of all the existing agreements between states, while planning interbasin transfers. Another distinct feature of the NPP is that the transfer of water is essentially by gravity and only in small reaches by lifts not exceeding 120m. The scheme was prima facie found to be technically feasible and economically viable when compared to the present cost of development of irrigational facilities.

The National Perspective Plan comprises of two components viz. Himalayan Rivers Development and Peninsular Rivers Development.

(*a*) **Himalayan Rivers Development:** Himalayan Rivers Development envisages construction of storage reservoirs on the principal tributaries of the Ganga and the Brahamaputra in India, Nepal and Bhutan, along with inter-linking canal systems to transfer surplus flows of the eastern tributaries of the Ganga to the west, apart from linking of the main

Brahamaputra and its tributaries with the Ganga and Ganga with Mahanadi.

(*b*) **Peninsular Rivers Development:** This component is divided into four major parts:

(*i*) Interlinking of Mahanadi-Godavari-Krishna-Cauvery-Vaigai rivers and building storages at potential sites in these basins.

(*ii*) Interlinking of west flowing rivers, north of Mombay and south of Tapi.

(*iii*) Interlinking of Ken-Chambal Rivers

(*iv*) Diversion of other west flowing rivers towards eastern side.

The National Perspective Plan would give additional benefits of 25 million ha of irrigation from surface waters, 10 million ha by increased use of ground waters, totaling to 35 Mha which will be over and above the ultimate irrigation potential of 140 million ha and 34,000 MW of hydro-power, apart from the benefits of flood control, mitigation of drought, navigation, domestic and industrial water supply, recreational facilities, salinity and pollution control etc.

National Water Development Agency

National Water Development Agency (NWDA) was set up in July, 1982 as an Autonomous Society under the Societies Registration Act, 1860 in the Ministry of Water Resources to carry out the water balance and other studies on a scientific and realistic basis to prepare feasibility reports for interbasin water transfer link schemes and thus to give concrete shape to Peninsular and Himalayan Rivers Development Components of NPP envisaging diversion of water from surplus basins to deficit/drought prone areas. The proposal includes construction of storage reservoirs to store flood waters and interlinking of river systems for optimum utilization of available water resources. The water so diverted will be used for irrigation, drinking and other uses.

The interlinking proposals comprises of three major links:

(*i*) First major link is the Southern Water Grid interlinking Mahanadi, Godavari, Krishna, Pennar, Cauvery and Vaigai in the Peninsular India to transfer surplus waters of Mahanadi and Godavari to deficit areas to benefit Orissa, Andhra Pradesh, Karnataka, Pondicherry and Tamil Nadu.

The other two links are the northern links.

(*ii*) Inter-linking Brahamaputra with Ganga, Subernarekha and Mahanadi to transfer surplus water of Brahamaputra to benefit areas in Assam, West Bengal, Bihar, Jharkhand and Odissa.

(*iii*) Interlinking Gandak, Ghagara, Sarda and Yamuna, all tributaries of Ganga, on to Rajasthan and Sabarmati to transfer the surplus waters of Gandak and Ghagara rivers to benefit areas in Uttar Pradesh, Uttaranchal, Haryana, Rajasthan, Gujarat, Bihar and Jharkhand.

Ultimately the Himalayan linkages from Brahamaputra to Ganga would be integrated with the peninsular link from Mahanadi to Vaigai.

Large dams and canal systems are proposed to be constructed to store and tansfer flood waters of the surplus rivers. For transferring surplus waters of Mahanadi and Godavari, dams are proposed to be constructed at Manibhadra on Mahanadi and Inchampalli and Polavarm on Godavari rivers.

Similarly, dams on Manas and Sankosh in Brahamaputra basin are proposed for storing and transferring water.

Apart from the three major links, a number of minor links are also proposed:

- Transferring surplus waters of Kosi to Mechi in the east and Ghagara in the west to benefit West Bengal, Bihar and U.P.
- Transferring water from Ken river to Betwa river to benefit Madhya Pradesh and Uttar Pradesh.
- Interlinking Parbati, Kalisindh and Chambal rivers to benefit area of Rajasthan and Madhya Pradesh.
- Interlinking of west flowing rivers north of Mumbai and south of Tapi to benefit Maharashtra and Gujarat.
- Transferring water from west flowing rivers of Western Ghats to the east to benefit Karnataka, Tamil Nadu and Kerala.

Interlinking of rivers would greatly reduce the regional imbalance in the availability of water in the different river basins. Surplus water which are flowing waste to sea would be fruitfully utilized. It is assessed that it will provide additional irrigation benefit to 35 Mha (25 Mha from surface water and additional 10 Mha from increased ground water recharge) which will be over and above the ultimate irrigation potential of 140 Mha envisaged from the conventional irrigation projects.

Normally all irrigation projects are planned for 75% dependability of water that is to say that these projects would be able to deliver the required quantity of water in 75 out of 100 years. The same approach has been adopted for the inter-basin water transfer projects.

Construction of storage dams as proposed will reduce the severity of floods and at the same time reduce flood damages considerably. The flood peaks are estimated to reduce by about 20 to 30% in Ganga and Brahamaputra basins.

The benefits of drought mitigation from interbasin water transfers will accrue to an area of about 25 lakh ha in the states of West Bengal, Bihar, Uttar Pradesh, Haryana, Rajasthan, Jharkhand, Madhya Pradesh, Gujarat, Andhra Pradesh, Karnataka and Tamil Nadu.

Huge capacity of hydro-power could also be generated by the storage dams proposed under interlinking of rivers. Hydro-power development has not kept pace with the potential and requirement in our country. Against 84,000 MW of potential, only about 22,000 MW of capacity for hydro-power generation has been developed so far. For efficient working of electrical energy generating system, the mix of thermal to hydro should be about 60:40. In our country it is about 75:25. The storage dams proposed under interlinking of rivers will greatly improve this situation. The total hydro-power potential of the interlinking systems will be 34,000 MW.

The mega cities of India and urban centres are already water short. Many of the metropolitan cities depend upon long distance inter-basin transfer of water for their domestic and industrial water supply. Delhi gets parts of its water supplies from Ganga and Sutlej, Mumbai gets water from Vaitarna and Batsai over a distance of 100 km, Chenai water supply is being augmented from Srisailam on Krishna which is 500 km away. Major part of future requirements of big cities will have to be met from long distance inter-basin transfer of water. In the link proposals under study by NWDA, water supply to Mumbai and Delhi cities and many other villages and habitations enroute the link canals are proposed to be augmented.

Most of the link canals will be 50 to 100 metres wide and more than 6 metres deep. That would greatly facilitate inland navigation from the north to deep south and attract tourism.

Programme of Completion of Feasibility Reports by NWDA

Based on the numerous water balance studies, toposheet studies of reservoir sites and link alignments etc., NWDA has identified in all 30 links for preparation of feasibility reports in line with the proposals of NPP. Out of these, 14 are under Himalayan Component and 16 under Peninsular Component.

Preparation of pre-feasibility reports for all link proposals has been completed by NWDA. The feasibility reports of 8 links have been completed. The surveys and investigations for preparation of feasibility reports of 16 links are at various stages of progress. It is programmed to complete feasibility studies of all the identified water transfer link schemes within 10 years.

In this context, the advantages and disadvantages of interlinking of the rivers in India can be put forth as follows:

Advantages

- The National Perspective Plan would give additional benefits of 25 million ha of irrigation from surface waters, 10 million ha by increased use of ground waters, raising the ultimate irrigation potential from 113 million ha to 148-150 million ha and generation of 34 million KW of power, apart from the benefits of flood control, navigation, water supply, fisheries, salinity and pollution control, etc.

Disadvantages

- The Himalayan and the Peninsular rivers have flood flows estimated at 30,000 to 60,000 cubic metres of water per second (cusec) during a few weeks in the monsoon season. But finer analysis reveals that only 4,500 cusecs is to be lifted from a total flood flow of

60,000 cusecs. Quite obviously lifting such small proportions will not mitigate, the country's flood problem specially in the southern peninsula.

- Interlinking is hardly justified as the solution for this problem. Moreover, it will be almost impossible to take the water to all the habitations without huge investments in a centralized distribution network.
- The World Bank estimates the health costs of water pollution in India to be equivalent to three per cent of the country's gross domestic product. With Indian rivers being severely polluted, interlinking them may actually increase these costs. Also, with the widely recognized failure of the Ganga Action Plan, there is a danger that contaminants from the Ganga basin might enter into other basins and destroy their natural cleansing processes. The new areas that will be river-fed after the introduction of the scheme may experience crop failures or routing due to alien compounds carried into their streams from the polluted Ganga basin streams.
- The costs of interlinking is estimated to be over Rs. 5,60,000 crore. But this is a conservative figure. The government suggested that it can raise money through loans, taxes and user charges. This means that local users will have to bear the enormous costs of sustaining the project. Interlinking rivers might thus end up creating illusions of water security, while in reality it will create conditions where privatization becomes the only alternative.
- The Himalaya and the Peninsula have flood flow estimates at 30,000 to 60,000 cubic metres of water per second during a few weeks in the monsoon season.

- The plan envisions tapping these flows, storing them in reservoirs and finally draining them over thousands of distributories.
- But finer analysis reveals that 4500 cusecs is to be lifted from a total flood flow of 60,000 cusecs. Quite obviously lifting such small proportions will not mitigate the country's flood problems.
- Transferring water might end up creating rancour between states and the centre. Because constitutionally also water remains in the state list.

Population of India is already over a billion now, which is expected to increase to 1500-1800 million by the year 2050. This would require about 450 million tons of food grains to support the increased population. It is imperative therefore to increase irrigation potential to 160 million hectares for all crops by 2050, which may not be possible through conventional water resources developmental activities. The basic irrigation facilities in India are substantially dependent on ground water. The declining trend of ground water level is a matter of serious concern. Per capita water storage capacity in India is also very low viz-a-viz the global scenario. Monsoon water flow into the sea is substantially high. We must therefore evolve a comprehensive and holistic approach on this issue.

Increase in irrigation facilities, will substantially supplement our poverty alleviation efforts, leading to expansion in job opportunities. However, the overall plan allocation for irrigation has reduced from 23% to 15% from the 1st Plan till now. Therefore, we must respond positively with a substantially higher allocation for irrigation before the start of the next Five Year Plan. Thus, other options including Inter-basin Transfer of Water are to be thought of, for providing water for meeting the ever increasing demand for food, and also to overcome regional imbalances in water availability. Inter-basin transfer of water is already being practiced in other countries like, China, USA and Canada. In China, a project for transfer of 48 BCM water from Yangtze river to another basin is almost complet. In the USA, 45 BCM of water has already been transferred, from the North California basin to the South California basin. Similarly, in Canada 268 BCM of water has been transferred from one basin to the other.

The UPA government headed by Dr. Manmohan Singh was inclined to the concept of Inter-basin Transfer of Water. The National Common Minimum Programme (NCMP) emphasizes the need of 'Interlinking of Rivers' but in a systematic manner. We are therefore making a comprehensive assessment of the feasibility of linking the rivers of the country, starting with the Peninsular rivers, in a fully consultative manner. It is assured that no attempt will be taken to muzzle the voice dissidents on the concept of this issue, rather dialogue and interaction with experts, social activists and NGOs shall continue for a conclusive status.

●●●

Chapter 5

Interbasin Transfer of Water

India, with its geographical area (329 million hectare) consisting only 2.45 percent of the earth's land mass, supports a population of about 1027 million (year 2001 census) which is about 16 percent of the earth's population. The renewable fresh water resource of India, at 1869 Billion Cubic Meter (BCM)/year, is only about 4 percent of the earth's water resources. Average Indian has hardly one - sixth of the land and one -fourth of water as compared to world average. In view of the severe is inevitable to ensure comfortable living to the people of India.

During 1950, we had reached a population of 400 million. That was the stage when India faced severe food crises as major food producing region in Indus basin went to Pakistan. India had to live on imported food, which was otherwise, usable as cattle feed in developed countries. Thanks to the great leaders of the nation who realized the need of the food security and launched massive programmes of irrigation through projects like Bhakra, which they called as temples of modern India. Ground water development was also intensified. This improvement helped the country from a state of food inadequacy to that of food sufficiency. This revolution has long since plateaued.

A large number of dams for irrigation were planned in this phase of 1950 to 2000. All favourable sites for dam construction have been exhausted. We are left with more difficult dam sites now. This has resulted in slow down of irrigation development. In fact, a stage of near stagnation been increasing. So also is the growing desire for improved standard of living resulting in continuous increase in the demand for food grains and water. The future could be grave, if immediate timely actions are not taken to ensure adequate food supply and safe drinking water over a larger time span.

In our India precipitation is the only source of fresh water supply. It has been constant over the last few centuries and will continue to be so for years to come. Unfortunately, the quality of water is not well protected. Man, through his behiviour and action is polluting the precious water and turning God's gift into 'Amrit' and preserve fresh water from turning God's gift into 'Amrit' and preserve fresh water from turning poisonous 'Amrit' is, therefore, required to conserve and protect the life giving and life sustaining qualities of water.

In an attempt to meet our growing needs, man started using the ground water, which had accumulated for centuries as the country could manage with available surface water. Recent ground water pumping, however, has resulted into mining and lowering of ground water for hundreds of feet, with the result that concentrated fluorides, nitrates, salinity and arsenic have reached dangerous levels in many areas making it unsafe for human consumption. Agriculture pumping, uncontrolled by any administrative or legal measures, has not only reduced the natural flows, but lowered its quality with ever increasing pollution.

India through this **Amrit Kranti** needs to put water to the best use of mankind. A major impending crisis has to be averted through **Water Sector Reforms** including demand management. This is the need of the day for the nation to ensure water security to our future generations.

Many projects of national importance have suffered due to differences between basin states. Such a situation would not have arisen if India was a unitary State or State boundaries were co-terminus with water basin boundaries. We, therefore, need to think in this direction, in term of water resources development of each basin for common good. There are instances of co-operation and good-will where basin States have agreed to spare water for non-basin State. Sardar Sarovar is one such example where **M.P., Gujrat** and **Maharashtra** agreed to spare water for Rajasthan. Unfortunately, the same States have diffculty in sorting out common issues. Can such issues be not resolved with the same spirit of co-operation and understanding without waiting for enabling constitutional and legal amendments?

Improved water management in agriculture, industry, domestic use only yield at least 10 to 15 percent of a additional availability. There is scope for improvement in all sectors. However, some would point finger at intensive water use in irrigation. Others say that in urban area, filtered and chlorinated water suitable for drinking is used to flush toilets and that the quantum used is more than what is available in rural areas for all uses. This is in addition to distribution losses which are also significant. Industries and cities are blamed for releasing untreated or partly treated industrial and domestic waste water, causing pollution. The need is to ensure improvement in all sectors of water use, not only for the benefit of others, but for their own benefit and that of their children.

Other water conservation measures like roof top and rain water harvesting, groundwater recharge, watershed management through check dams etc. have all a role to play, particularly in areas which are not likely to derive benefit from flow irrigation, through large storages. Water conservation measures could be used to meet needs in such cases. In low rainfall areas and drought prone pockets, their effectiveness is not significant but they can provide partial relief.

Annual precipitation including snowfall in the country has been 4000 BCM for centuries and will remain nearly the same for centuries to come barring radical climate change. Groundwater is a part of the surface water which percolates into ground. At places, the same groundwater reappears as surface water so pumped again returns to ground after application for irrigation and other uses. Same is true for surface water applied for irrigation and other uses. The water entering into ground, sometimes percolates into deep aquifers and/or mixes with low quality underground water and saline strata, rendering it unsuitable or uneconomical for reuse. Surface water, right from the stage it falls as rain till it finally drains into the sea is subjected to evaporation. The hydrological cycle is thus complex but the final outcome is that out of annual precipitation of 4000 BCM, 1869 BCM is all that is available as fresh water while the rest is lost in evaporation etc. or escapes into sea during the floods. To the extent we can store this this flood water, we can augment lean season supplies. This is possible only through large storages. The present availability of utilisable surface and ground water which is at 1122 BCM/wili have to be stretched to meet the requirements of an anticipated popultion of 1640 million by year 2050.

Geographical area of India is 329 million ha and net cultivable area is 143 million ha, for a population of 1027. In this ratio, one million ha land, would have about 4,40/00 ha of cultivable land and population of 3 million. If the rainfall of the area is 100 mm, which is the case in some areas, cultivation would be possible only in monsoon. The cultivable land can optimistically produce about 4,40/000 tonnes against requirement of 8/50/000 tonnes food.

It is a paradox that in India, some areas are precariously facing inadequacy of water resources, whereas there are others, which receive huge supplies, in excess of the genuine requirement of the population they support. This not only results in devastating floods which ruin large areas but also pours huge volumes of water into sea.

For protection against drought it is necessary to augment water supply through transport of water from water surplus regions, through interlinking of rivers and interbasin transfers. This is not to say that other augmentation techniques such as rain water harvesting, recharges of ground water, watershed management etc. will not be adopted. All these measures are complementary and would supplement each other, and none is to the exclusion of the other. Thus all these options should form part ofthe overall water resources development package.

Through the wisdom of planners and politicians, many drought prone areas, particularly in the North West (Punjab, Haryana, and Northern Rajasthan) as also some irrigated patches in the south have been drought proofed through this strategy of bringing water from outside area. Even then, large tracts of such areas remain unprotected. In order to make these areas achieve some measure of self sufficiency in food, reasonable levels of income & employment opportunities for their rural-agricultural based population, such drought proofing through irrigation becomes a desirable national target. A map showing the drought districts of India is at Plate-I

India has agricultural base and the most of its population lives in villages. The rural areas therefore need to be helped, through augmentation of supplies to meet the basic need of domestic supply and support agriculture, to make the rural base stronger. Drought proofing, with, whatever measures, economically affordable and sustainable have to be thought of and practised. Each of the drought proofing measure has its own merits and demerits and limitations and clearly appreciating these, the same need to be prioritized and implemented in efforts to stabilize rural economy and further develop it to the extent possible.

STRATEGIES FOR WATER DEVELOPMENT

For the meeting the target of water withdrawal requirements for various uses, it is apparent that various developmental strategies based on micro macro actions, and prioritizing either ground or surface water development would need to be considered. Water would need to be conserved through various measures from the point it falls as rainfall till it drains into the sea. Such measures could be watershed management, rainwater harvesting, groundwater recharge, check dams, small and medium storages etc. These measures are useful for tapping the local rainfall though their performance is severely affected in low rainfall areas during droughts, when protection is most needed. The entire water falling within that area could not meet its genuine needs. The water requirements for all uses are so large that a single development strategy cannot meet these on its own. The National Commission for Integrated Water Resources Development Plan (NCIERDP) has also expressed the view that in a basin plan, there must be a place for a whole range of structures, large to small. Large dams enable storages of large volumes of water which can be carried long distances and used all year round. This is not possible in small structures. The small structures have localized benefits and applications, whereas large storages have a capability to transfer water over longer distances. Thus, interbasin transfer of water as a concept emerges as an important strategy in the overall development of Water Resources scenario in the country.

The ultimate irrigation potential of the country is assessed as 140 million hectares-76 million ha from surface water and 64 million ha from ground water. This may become substantially short for meeting projected food requirements by 2050 AD. Shortages and large scale of import of food grain is likely to be socially unacceptable even in a globalised economy. This makes it imperative to look for other nonconventional methods of increasing irrigation potential. Interbasin water transfer based on proven technology has a potential of 35 million ha of additional irrigation enhancing total ultimate irrigation to 175 million ha. Food is expected to be the weapon of tomorrow in international scenario. Attempts, therefore, need to be made not only to be satisfied with producing enough to eat, but the strategy need to be to produce surpluses for export to achieve a commanding position. Therefore, considering both internal consumption and export, the country has to plan for 550 million tonnes of food grain production by 2050 AD.

Long distance interbasin transfer of water is not a new concept and has been in practice in India for over five centuries. The Periyar Project, Parambikulam Aliyar Project, Kurnool-Cudappah canal & The Telugu Ganga Project are good examples of interbasin water transfers executed in South India in the 19th & 20th centuries. **The Periyar Project** is the most notable endeavour of the 19th century in transbasin diversion. A masonry gravity dam 47.28 m high was constructed across a gorge on the west flowing Periyar river. A 1740m long tunnel with a discharging capacity of 40.75m^3/waters eastwards to the Vaigai basin. The project was commissioned in 1895 and provided irrigation to 0.58 lakh ha initially, which has since been extended to 0.81 lakh ha. There is also a power station of 140 MW capacity. **Parambikulam Aliyar Project** is a complex multi-basin multi-purpose project. Seven streams, five flowing towards west and two towards the east, have been damed and their reservoirs interlinked by tunnels. The water is ultimately delivered to drought prone areas in Coimbatore district of Tamil Nadu and Chittur area of Kerala State. The project has a command areas of 1.62 lakh ha and a total of 185 MW of power generation capacity. The Kurnool-Cuddapah canal is 304 km long with a capacity of 84,9m^3/s extending from Krishna to Pennar basin for irrigationg an area of 0.53 lakh ha. The Telugu **Ganga Project** brings Krishana waters from Srisailam reservoir through an open canal, first to Somasila reservoir in Pennar valley. From Somasila, water is taken through a 45 km canal to Kandaleru and then to Poondi reservoir in Tamil Nadu through another 200 km long canal. By agreement among the riparian States 12 TMC of water delivered to Tamil Nadu to augment water supply to Chennai city. The canal also irrigates 2.33 lakh ha in Andhra Pradesh enroute.

Similarly in North India, inter sub-basin transfer in the Indus basin and Rajasthan canal project are some of the projects excuted in the 19th & 20th centuries. Inter sub -basin Transfer in the Indus Basin: A diversion dam, Pandoh, 140 km upstream of Pong Dam on Beas, enables diversion of water from Beas to Bhakra reservoir on Sutlej river and generates 165 MW of power on the way. The Beas-Sutlej link is 37.25 km long of which 25.45 km is tunnel through difficult rock formations. The Indira Gandhi Canal diverts water from the Himalayas to the deserts of the Rajasthan. The project comprises of a huge multi purpose project constructed across the Beas river at Pong, through barrages at Harike and a grand canal system. These interlinking projects executed both in South and North India have been highly beneficial and have not resulted in any noticeable environmental damages.

●●●

Chapter 6

The Myth and Reality

Yes, there are several questions standing in the way of Inter-linking the Indian Rivers. Not only engineers, politicians, bureaucrats, journalists, historians and philosophers have joined hands to question the practibility of the project. Some senior experts and experienced persons of national and international repute, such as Prof. Rama Swamy R. Iyer, Dr. Bharat Singh, Dr. M.S. Reddy, Sudhirendra Sharma, J.N. Godrej, B.S. Raghavan and Dr. Saumitra Mukherjee raised doubts regarding the desirability and viability of this ambitious project.

Objecting the idea Er. Sudhirendra said (former Chairman CWC). The proposed interlinking of all the major rivers of the country is but a supermarket approach to meeting all the basic needs–of drinking water, irrigation and power–at one go. It is also a perfect political tool to woo the electorate, the opposition to which has been hard to come by. For a minority of the conscientious citizens though, this has been the greatest contemporary challenge the governing elite has posed.

Though several times the combined impact of all major development projects in the country, the river-linking initiative has been presented as the panacea for all the conceivable ills. Inconceivable benefits notwithstanding, it could initiate the kind of growth that offers cover for rampant corruption and lucrative kickbacks.

The recent cases of corruption in the Environment Ministry are clear indications that ecological and environmental concerns are taking a back seat. The coalition of political opportunism brushes aside instances of corruption as mere exceptions, ignoring the fact that such 'exceptions' are indeed threatening to become 'rules'. The inevitable side effects of development have indeed been taken for granted.

Ecological Ignorance

The interlinking of rivers is being projected as one giant move to complete nature's unfinished agenda. With surplus flow into the Brahamaputra and less-than-desired flow into the Cauvery being the overriding concerns, the governing elite intends to bring equality in water access across the diverse eco-regions of the country.

How can nature allow one river basin to be water-rich and not the others? By 2050, the per capita availability in the Brahamaputra basin would be 9,000 kilolitres against 400 for the peninsular basins of Cauvery and Pennar.

Short-circuiting nature through inter-basin transfer may seem technologically feasible and, in a sense, possible too. But if that were really so, the mighty Indus could have easily flowed through the desert of Rajasthan into the sea via the shortest route and the same would be applicable to the Brahamaputra as well.

Not only is ecology being undermined, geography too seems to be at the receiving end. Unprecedented in the country's independent history, both are being altered without getting the conventional nod from the protectors of our Constitution.

Surplus flow and its wasteful discharge into the oceans seem the prime movers for the project. What if the food (the elusive calcium molecule that travels from the mountain slopes) does not reach the corals in the sea?

Even considering the country's projected demand in 2050, the current supply is enough to meet the need for 1,447 bcm of water of an estimated 1.64 billion population. Much cheaper eco-friendly options are being bypassed in favour of this proposal that will cost the country well over $500 billion, factoring in cost escalations and anticipated delays.

Political Arrogance

Ecological ignorance coupled with political arrogance is well reflected in the statement by the Former Chairman of the Task Force on Interlinking of Rivers, Mr. Suresh Prabhu: "The Government doesn't have proprietary rights on 'wisdom', but the Government has the right to 'act' upon its decisions." But were not the decisions supposed to be people-centric? If so, why is peoples wisdom being discounted?

Not many know that the country's first Prime Minister did not allow the 'disease of gigantism' to trouble him for long. In a book Jawaharlal–A biography, Prof. S. Gopal records Nehru's subsequent views on the subject expressed at the Central Board of Irrigation & Power meeting on November 17, 1958: "Nehru was now more aware than in the past when, surveying the Bhakra-Nangal dam in 1956, he had whispered to himself, "These are the new temples of India where I worship."

Addressing the meeting, Pt. Nehru had remarked, "... (he) doubted very much if the Government would have initiated such a project if it came before them at this time. Such a dam was exceedingly expensive, involved a considerable amount of foreign exchange and took a long time to be completed. All that India had gained from it was electric power and little irrigation."

Interestingly, Dr. K.L. Rao, whose Ganga-Cauvery link plan has been repackaged into the interlinking of rivers proposal, was a minister in Nehru's Cabinet.

History repeated itself when Rajiv Gandhi, speaking to State Irrigation Ministers in August 1986, said: "The situation today is that since 1951, 246 big surface irrigation projects have been completed, 151 are still under construction.

Perhaps, we can safely say that almost no benefit has come to the people from these projects. For 16 years, we have poured out money. The people have got nothing back, no irrigation, no water, no increase in production, no help in their daily life."

Any decision that could affect the lives of millions must go through the rigour of scrutiny of all the available documents on the subject.

Collective Avarice

The interlinking of rivers proposal offers the politician electoral gains, as votes can still be bargained for false promises. For industry, the interlinking promises consumption of cement and steel for decades. For bureaucrats, it presents opportunity to barter contracts. And for engineering and other professionals, it will be a dream come true.

The promise that the proposal will generate 34,000 MW of power; extent irrigation to dry districts in the country and boost GDP by 4 per cent sounds good on paper. If the track record of past projects is any indication, it is an illusion that has been successfully sustained through the past six decades of our independent existence.

According to an analysis made by Shri B.S. Raghavan– "Any impartial assessment has been made difficult by the non-availability to any impartial body outside the government of the full documentation and data gathered by the NWDA.

They are being kept under wraps ostensibly on the ground that every thing pertaining to the water system of the Himalayan region, closely watched as it is by India's suspicious neighbours of China, Bangladesh, Myanmar (Burma), Nepal and Bhutan, are confidential. The unsettling, if slightly comical, fact is that the contending technical lobbies are pleading the relative merits of their approaches purely based on theoretical assumptions on the contents of the NWDA'S feasibility study.

The case made out by the NWDA and the passionate official and non-official votaries of the project has been undermined by another creature of the government, the National Commission for Integrated Water Resources Development, throwing yet another spanner into the works.

After taking account of the average potential of all the rivers in India, the ultimately utilizable flow, the growth in population as well as norms for better standards of living, and the estimated and projected water demand for India by 2050 for all conceivable purposes, the Commission has asseverated that this demand can be fully met from available surface and ground water resources with appropriate measures for development and management without the need for any large-scale inter-basin transfer. What it all amounts to is that paralysis by analysis having set in, the possibility of reconciling the engineering aspects of the projects any time soon seems remote.

There is no agreement on the cost estimate either. The amount of Rs. 5,60,000 crore given to the Supreme Court as a ball-park figure is forbiddingly awesome. It pales into insignificance before another computation made by a team in the Institute of Engineers. According to its report, factoring the capital recovery cost, interest and inflation during the long 20 year period of construction, it will cost precisely Rs. 20, 17, 468 crore, coming roughly to Rs. 1 lakh crore a year. The team has worked out the annual capital recovery cost of electricity alone at 7 per cent interest over 50 years to be Rs. 13.3 per watt. The computation may or may not merit acceptance, but it makes out a case for realistic financial scrutiny which has been wanting...."

The political class and public opinion too are divided on the proposal to link rivers as between water-starved and (supposedly) surplus States. States through which major perennial rivers flow are in no mood to allow diversion of any quantity as, in their view, the water is inadequate even to meet their own projected future requirements. Just to mention the modest 51-km Pampa-Achenkoil-Vaippar link which will submerge only an inconsequential area of 1700 hectares and involve no displacement of people, only the other day, the Kerala Chief Minister flatly ruled it out, saying that the two rivers originated and joined the sea well within the State's boundaries and were therefore its own property. When such is the possessiveness of States within the same country, it is going to be tough to assuage the genuine concerns of Nepal, China and Bhutan with regard to the Ganga and the Brahamaputra which have upper catchments in those countries and Bangladesh, which strongly feel that they have a stake and a say in waters of these rivers.

Going ahead will also mean taking on the vociferous environmentalist and human rights outfits which are worried over the disturbance of the eco-systems of river basins and displacement of large numbers of people.

It is clear that the project bristles with too many assumptions and loose ends. On present showing, as the National Commission for Integrated Water Resources Development sums it up, "There seems to be no imperative necessity for massive water transfers. The assessed needs of the basins could be met from full development and efficient utilization of intra-basin resources except in the case of the Cauvery and the Vaigai basins. Therefore, it is felt that limited water transfer from the Godavari at Ichampalli and Polavaram towards the south would take care of the deficit in the Cauvery and the Vaigai basins."

Former Union Minister Som Pal opined–Technical feasibility apart, the immense investment and energy needed would not be commensurate with the potential benefit.

No less important are the political and legal problems. The way various states have been quarrelling with each other over water, flouting not only the tribunal awards but also the apex court orders, poses a serious question mark on the feasibility of the project.

The moot point is whether there could be a viable approach to solving the water problem. The Tenth Plan has presented a sceanario. According to the Plan, there were 383 ongoing major and medium projects awaiting completion, 88 of which are pending since pre-fifth Plan period i.e. more than 36 years. All these can be completed within five to eight years, yielding an additional potential of about 14 million hectares at a cost of Rs. 77,000 crore as estimated by the plan task force, now raised to Rs. 100,000 crore. The second component listed in the Plan is development of minor irrigation, mostly in the eastern and north eastern regions. The total potential assessed is 24.5 million hectares with a total investment of Rs. 54,000 crore, of which the government is expected to provide only Rs. 13,500 crore, the balance coming from beneficiary farmers and institutional loans.

The success of such a scheme has clearly been demonstrated in Assam, where only 33,000 tubewells, of the planned 100,000, have helped the perennially foodgrain deficit state become surplus one within two to three years. The cost per hectare is only Rs. 20,000 and gestation period almost nil, against a cost of Rs. 100,000 and 12 years' gestation in case of major and medium projects. The annual rainfall in the region, ranging from 1,200 mm to 5,000 mm, is enough to keep the groundwater regularly recharged. Most of the tubewells being shallow, the cost of installation and power consumption would be low. The third equally beneficial scheme mentioned in the Plan is the groundwater recharge master plan prepared by the Central Ground Water Board needing Rs. 24,500 crore to trap 36 billion cubic metres of water annually. The Plan, however, has allocated only paltry sums for this exercise.

There is a readily available alternative which can create about 50 million hectares of irrigation potential in five to eight years with an investment of Rs. 1,38,000 crore. Legal, environmental, resettlement and distributional issues either do not arise or have been settled. On the other hand, there is a far-fetched plan requiring Rs. 5,60,000 crore expected to yield only 25 million hectare irrigation and fraught with so many insurmountable problems. The choice seems clear.

J N Godrej says–'The nation cannot afford to take any hasty decision about the river-linking project as the ecological, economic and social stakes involved are too high'.

Five criteria were suggested, at a UNESCO workshop on inter-basin water transfer in April 1999 at Paris, by Prof.. William E Cox, of the Virginia Tech University, for justifying or rejecting the transfers. First, the receiving area must face substantial deficit in meeting present or projected future water demands after considering alternative supply sources and all reasonable measures for reducing demand. Second, water resources and all reasonable measures for reducing demand. Third, substantial environmental damage should not occur in the area of origin or area of delivery, to be substantiated by a comprehensive environment impact assessment study. Fourth, no substantial socio-cultural disruptions should result in either the area of origin or delivery, to be substantiated by a detailed socio-cultural impact assessment study. Finally, the benefits of inter-basin transfer should be equitably shared between the area of delivery and origin.

If this checklist contains five ticks, then river inter-linking should not be an issue in India. Unfortunately, it is. Not surprisingly, environmental groups have sounded most of the caveats against the plan to network India's Himalayan and Peninsular rivers.

In fact, environmental experts are of the opinion that floods– that the river-linking project seeks to prevent–are not necessarily a bad proposition in the long run. The logic is that natural flood cycles result in the deposition of alluvium, essential for maintaining soil fertility. Any process like building dams and reservoirs, which prevents this natural process, will cause land fertility to deteriorate gradually, turning cultivable land into wastelands. Recent floods in Europe clearly indicate that some of the flood preventive measures–embankments, canalization of rivers–are the root causes of floods. It is also being emphasized that the United States and Europe are now investing billions of dollars to revive some rivers and remove dams and embankments.

Of course, there is an equally persuasive lobby in favour of river inter-linking arguing that it isn't just about preventing floods and droughts. It is linked to global climatic change. The major river basins like that of the Ganga and Brahamaputra are fed by glacial waters from the Himalayas. The impact of climate change on glaciers is quite compelling and the glacial retreat over the years would mean severe shortage of freshwater availability in the fertile plains of the Ganga basin. Initially, the effect may be severe flooding but with complete retreat of the glaciers there will be reduced water flow leading to lack of water availability. Under the circumstances river inter-linking will have no real value.

The lobby for river-linking feels that such projects link the regions with surplus water to ones with acute shortage. Staunch proponents argue that the project is necessary for increasing the irrigated land area to meet future food demand. This is needed to prepare for the consequences of climate change on water resources.

But there is a school of thought that argues that increased acreage of land under cultivation will lead to increased fertiliser use and increased production of gases affecting the global climate.

However, the concept of inter-basin water transfer has been in practice for the past five centuries. The western Yamuna canal and Agra canal build during Mughal times are examples. Let us side-step the tussle for and against the environmental impact of the river-linking project and just drive home four simple messages on river inter-linking.

- We must assess the ecological and social costs of river inter-linking through an independent and credible process.
- Learn from others' experience. There are several examples of inter-basin transfers such as Aral Sea, Karnaganda Canal, GAP project in Turkey and the most-recent controversies about the Spanish hydrological plan and China's south-north diversion. India can benefit from some of the analysis of those projects.
- Explore alternatives to meet the same goal. In India, several imaginative and proven solutions were developed–rainwater harvesting, watershed manage-ment, etc. But they need investments to see the benefits at the national level.

After all this analysis if the inter-linking of rivers is the only option then everyone will support it. Also nobody should be able to tell us that we didn't do our homework. The benefits of inter-linking should exceed its ecological and social costs. To start with, the post-networking impact on the environment needs to be carefully isualised and assessed with the help of simulation models, developed along with geological and morphological studies.

The practical solutions need to be carefully framed taking care to ensure that existing bridges and barrages across rivers are not affected by post-networking phenomenon like riverbed retrogression, excessive sedimentation and erratic channel drifting. Then there are the issues of glaciation to be flashed out. Remember, three main rivers: Ganga, Brahamaputra and the Indus rely on water from glacial sources. In depth studies on the glacial structure–pre-and networking–must therefore be put in place.

Dr. Bharat Singh a senior technocrat has seen no justification in the project and argue that–It seems a little odd that the present initiative for inter-linking of rivers came not from the Planning Commission nor from National Water Resources Development Council but from the Supreme Court who were primarily considering drinking water problems. By the Government's own claims, more than 80% of the country's population has already been provided with safe drinking water. The quantity required to meet the remaining domestic needs is so small that it cannot justify the mammoth river inter-linking project. We are already producing enough food, the production can be further increased by at least 25% from existing irrigated area itself by improved inputs and agricultural technology. Any water resources engineer will immediately discard inter-linking of rivers as a flood control measure. Yet the Government of India almost immediately endorsed the Supreme Court direction and gave a time span of 12 years for implementation. In view of the fact that we have been taking more than 20 years for completion of single high dam projects, the time seems totally unrealistic. Looking at the on going disputes between states, inter-state agreements would be extremely difficult to achieve. There really seems to be no convincing argument or vital national interest which can justify undertaking this mammoth undertaking in its entirety.

Questioning the very basics of this project Prof. R.R. Iyer stated–The notion of the linking of the rivers in the subcontinent is an old one. In the 19th century, Sir Arthur Cotton had thought of a plan to link rivers in southern India for inland navigation. The idea was partially implemented but was later abandoned because inland navigation lost ground to the railways. Even the canal that was constructed went into decline.

The program 'inter-linking of rivers' is also often referred to as 'inter-basin transfers'. Essentially, the thinking is that the disparities in the different river basins of India call for water transfers from the 'surplus' basins to the 'deficit' basins. This has exercised the minds of the Indian water-resource planners for a long-time.

Apart from considerations of techno-economic viability, on which the proposition was abandoned, the diversion of waters from the Ganga will have international implications. Bangladesh view this with apprehensions and raise objections.

Under the India-Bangladesh Treaty of December 1996 on the sharing of Ganga waters, India has undertaken to protect the flows arriving at Farakka, which is the sharing point. Bangladesh contends that a diversion of waters from the Ganga to the southern rivers will not be consistent with that undertaking. Besides, it is a proposition accepted by both India and Bangladesh that the Ganga is water-short in the lean season and needs to be 'augmented', though the two sides have different notions on the means of augmentation: that is a debatable proposition, but if that is in fact true, where is the scope for diversion from the Ganga?

Barring a few cases where short gravity links may be feasible, interbasin transfers generally involve the carrying of water across the natural barrier between basins by lifting, or by tunnelling through, or by a long circuitous routing around the mountains if such a possibility exists in a given case. Exceptionally heavy capital investments and continuing energy costs (in operation) are almost always likely to be involved. In addition, big dams, reservoirs and conveyance systems will need to be built, involving substantial environmental impacts and displacement/rehabilitation problems. All this will need to be looked at very closely in every case. Thorough Environmental Impact Assessments, Cost-Benefit analyses, qualitative assessments of non-quantifiable considerations, and based on these, rigorous investment appraisals, will need to be undertaken. Not too many projects are likely to survive such a scrutiny.

Even more serious is the funding problem. Plan outlays are barely adequate even for the completion of projects already undertaken. One estimate–that of the NCIWRDP–of amounts needed to complete spill-over projects is Rs. 70,000 crore in the Tenth Plan and Rs. 110,000 crore in the Eleventh Plan.

The Ministry of Water Resources at the Centre has for long been trying to enlarge its role, but has been finding this difficult because of resistance by the State bureaucracies. Against that background, the Supreme Court's direction on the linking of rivers must have been very welcome to it, because any such large national undertaking on inter-State rivers is bound to enlarge its role substantially. Not only is its 'clout' vis-a-vis the State bureaucracies likely to increase, but its relative importance among the Ministries at the Centre may also go up. Its position will be further strengthened if there is new legislation to underpin the river-linking idea.

In this regard Prof. Saumitra Mukherjee, after proper analysis stated that–socio-economic study and collection of environmental baseline data will form a key component of this river-linking project. The strong environmental activism against such colossal project is there and will be there. But this needs to be countered with proper scientific judgement and quality data. The success of this project has to be taken on the basis of proper mass awareness through mass media and involvement of selected NGO's. There has to be a third party scrutiny of the work of the NGOs to cut short the role of vested interest. The evaluation parameters have to be fixed. The benefit has to be highlighted to the masses through slide shows, pamphlets, mass awareness campaign etc. We will have to ensure local participation in the grass root level and ensure that the local knowledge is taken on board while making any positive decision.

The cost benefit analysis has to be proper and should not involve set parameters established by World Bank or any other donor agency but by parameters which are local and not based on evaluation parameters established for conditions alien to Indian condition.

I feel that the best approach is to select a small river basin and implement the scheme based on sound step by step approach. During this particular pilot scale approach we can fine tune our findings and learn whatever mistakes are being made and rectify during the course of this particular project. After a lapse of about a few years, if the results prove satisfactory the set model may be replicated for larger areas.

In the face of such opposition, India's Ex. Prime Minister Manmohan Singh has shown far less enthusiasm than former P.M., A.B. Vajpayee for the river-linking project and called for detailed techno-economic studies before finally committing himself one way or another.

Dr. Singh is troubled by serious inter-state water-sharing disputes such as that between Tamil Nadu and Karnataka in the South over the waters of the river Cauvery and the unilateral termination of earlier agreements by Punjab to share the waters of the Sutlej river with Haryana state.

At the international level Bangladesh has made it clear that it was against any unilateral plan by India to use artificial canals to divert waters from the Brahamaputra which originates in Tibet and has proposed an integrated water resources management plan that includes all coriparian countries including China, Bhutan and Nepal.

Sudhirendra Sharma, a former C'man C.W.C. and water expert with the World Bank and currently attached to the Delhi-based Ecological Foundation sees merit in Dhaka's demand for a regional approach to managing the subcontinent's water resources.

●●●

Chapter 7

Alternative Proposals

National Waterways Development Council, a Madurai-based NGO, has come out with an alternative proposal for networking rivers and viable solutions for its implementation.

NAWAD council chairman A C Kamaraj claimed that the Ganga-Cauvery National Waterways Project (NWP), connecting River Ganga and the Cauvery and also the Brahamaputra and the Thambaraparani up to Kanniyakumari, was also technically feasible and economically viable.

Kamaraj, also a member of the expert committee, task force on linking of rivers, said the Government need not struggle for funds for the project, which was to cost Rs. 5.35 lakh crore, as it could be executed under BOT (build, operate and transfer) basis.

The project envisaged construction of three waterways, namely 4,500-km-long Himalayan waterways, the 5,750-km-long Central waterways and 4,650-km-long Southern waterways. The tributaries of rivers would be intercepted by the three loop-canals for impounding water in the Himalayan, Central and Southern regions. The floods in a river passing through a state would be discharge into the canals instead of flowing into sea.

"The states will receive water from the canal during drought situations," he explained and added that they were planning to capture only 30 per cent of water flowing into the sea.

Listing out the advantages, Kamaraj said–"the NWP would bring in 150 million acres of land under irrigation. It would also help generation of pollution-free power to the tune of 60,000 MW, resulting in a revenue of Rs. 50,000 crore per annum."

The project also facilitate internal navigation throughout the year, refusing road transport. As a result, cost on oil import would be reduced by Rs. 65,000 crore per annum, he added.

Kamaraj claimed that the project had been appreciated by President A P J Abdul Kalam and had also evoked positive response from the independent group of experts, set up by the Ministry of Water Resources.

Many states, including Kerala, had evinced keen interest on NWP which could be completed in a period of 11 years, he said and added that the project was under the consideration of the Union Ministry of Water Resources and Planning Commission.

Alternative Proposal on Linking Forests and Rivers

In the outgoing water crisis it is more beneficial to link forests with river says Pandurang Hegde–

One of the main hypothesis of river linking is that the rivers in North India are perennial as they originate from the snow clad peaks or glaciers in the Himalayas.

The recent report of World Wildlife Fund for Nature, an international organization, has come out with the fact that "Himalayan glaciers are among the fastest receding in the world due to global warming and this will eventually lead to the drying up of glacier-fed rivers and causing water shortage in the Indian subcontinent." Obviously, with such a drastic prediction, the project to interlink rivers in India loses its rationale.

The rivers in India originate either from the glaciers in Himalayas or from the forests in the hill regions. As Chipko leader and noted environmentalist Sunderlal Bahuguna says,

"The forests are the mothers of rivers." The forests are the catchment areas of most of the rivers in our country. The mighty Ganga originates in Himalayas whereas the Cauvery and Krishna originate in the forest region of the Western Ghats.

These catchment forests serve the basic function of absorbing moisture from rainfall and assist in recharging the streams, which feed into our rivers. Essentially, the natural forests perform these functions effectively. Realising this primary function of the catchment forests and also to conserve these fragile forest ecosystems, people from time immemorial have made the sources of rivers as "sacred" and converted them into pilgrimage centres.

Thus, the Gangotri, (the origin of Ganga) or Tala Cauvery (the origin of Cauvery) are pilgrimage spots for us. The reverence to the origin, to the rivers and to the catchment forests is in built with the purpose of conserving these resources. Before the theme of conservation of origin of rivers had already evolved in our culture.

At present, we have jettisoned the culture of conservation of river catchments and we have adopted an approach which has not only destroyed the forests but also created a trail of destruction of water resources, our rivers and streams. In most parts of the country, the natural forests in the catchments of rivers are clearly felled to make way for monoculture plantations. In the Himalayas, the natural broad leaf Oak trees are felled to make way for Pine monoculture plantations. In Central India and Eastern regions, we have felled Sal forests to replace it with Teak monocultures.

Finally, in South India, in the Western Ghats, we have felled the most bio-diverse tropical forests to plant Teak and Eucalyptus plantations. Once, the group that walked along the River Sharavati in Karnataka found that almost eighty per cent of the catchment forests are planted with exotic acacia plantations.

This large-scale conversion of natural forests into monoculture plantations has had drastic impact on the river ecosystems as well as on the hydrology of the region.

Consequently, we see that most of the rivers that flow during the monsoon months, are red with the silt of the hilly region. This is an indicator of the dead river. Coupled with this is the fact that most rivers are polluted and water is not fit for human or animal consumption. The National Forest Policy recognizes the fact that forests need to be conserved for meeting the ecological functions and conservation of water resources in the country. The National Water Policy of the government does not even mention the link of forests to water resources. It takes for granted, the availability of water that needs to be supplied to various stake-holders. These crucial policy papers are devoid of looking at the important issues in a holistic manner.

The need of the hour is to re-establish the links between forests and water, to evolve the holistic approach to water crisis. It is essential and priority ought to be given to conservation of the natural catchment forests instead of converting them into monoculture plantations. In order to get assured perennial water supply in our rivers and streams, it is essential to go back to the wisdom of conserving our sources of water and rivers, the forests.

In our national anthem, we say "**sujalam**" and "**suphalam**", meaning the abundance of water for our countrymen. In reality, the country is facing one of the worst water crisis.

On the occasion of Water Day, it has been declared– "While celebrating the World Water Day, let us commit ourselves to conserving our watersheds of rivers and not pollute them. similarly, while celebrating the World Forestry Day, let us not look at the forests as the resource that provides us timber, but consider it as the nature's factory that provides the soil and water also."

●●●

Chattisgarh and West Bengal, a major reason for which is the lack of jobs, and improve national security.

It is well-known fact that India is blessed with good water resources in the form of rivers spanning 170 thousand km, water bodies over 68 million bectares and vast ground water resources. The annual utilization potential of surface water is estimated to be 690 billion cubic meters and the same for ground water is 432 billion cubic meters.

But much of this river water is wasted by flowing into the sea. While large part of Northern and Eastern India suffers from terrible floods every year, yet the other part of India continues suffering from drought. If India has to prosper, inter-linking the rivers is the most imperative.

We need to find a way to transfer water from surplus basins to deficit basins and this is what the Vajpayee Government was embarking upon. It is nobody's case that there are no pitfalls and problems, rather there are plenty of them. Anyone can imagine what types of difficulties successive Governments faced in constructing the Sardar Sarovar Dam. Ultimately, Supreme Court had to silence the agitation. Today millions are reaping the benefits of the dam. Bhakhra Nangal Dam too was questioned, but today its water is flowing up to Barmer and Jaisalmer in Rajasthan. This mega project addresses the problem of water resources in totality. The question of resources of about Rs. 7 lakh crore is also raised. Where would it come from? About 30 lakh people may even be displaced. Contrary to popular notion, migration and displacement ultimately results in economic betterment of the groups and socities who suffer the transition. Rivers are a very sensitive issue with local people as well as the States. We have witnessed the Cauveri dispute, a prickly problems in the relations between Karnataka and Tamil Nadu. Among the northern states, Punjab, Haryana and Rajasthan too are entangled in similar tensions. But these examples should not act as a deterrent for this mega project. Ecological and environmental issues are also raised, though not without basis. But quite often they are highly exaggerated. Eventually the project would address the problem of water scarcity wholesomely.

In the beginning of the 21 st century India has gathered the courage to solve the problem of water scarcity and turbulent floods just within two decades.

●●●

Chapter 9

Water Management–Social and Legal Aspects

The United Nations Report on Water for Life 2005-2015 estimates that one out of six people more than a billion population does not have adequate access to safe water. All major claims and conflicts over water in the world arise in respect of the share and distribution of three per cent of fresh water, which occurs in poles, glaciers, rivers, ponds and other waterbodies.

Access to water for all people was considered a primary need and given priority in governance during the pre-colonial days. Wells, tanks and other waterbodies were created and managed by people themselves with their traditional knowledge. Official data by the Archaeological Survey of India (ASI) reveal that 6,76,000 big structures for rainwater harvesting were in use, some of them 1,000 years old. They were constructed and maintained by villagers for their life and development. Water governance was articulated as an art and inherited by generation after generation as an integral part of life.

In India the present sovereign power over waterbodies and rivers is a concept introduced by British rulers and it prevented communities from participating in preserving the waterbodies for their proper use. The doctrine of public trust, which is embedded in the Constitution, had prevailed in India prior to the British administration. But the Northern India Canal and Drainage Act, 1873, the first law on water resources, introduced the state's right over water sources. Subsequently, other laws such as the Easements Act, 1882, which determines the right and ownership of private parties over enjoyment of water flow, were enacted. The British laws had minimized the participation of public-spirited people in water governance.

Since the adoption of the Constitution, water has become a State subject under List II. Hitherto, more than 32 Central Acts enacted by Parliament and two national water policies, 1987 and 2002, have been drafted. Consequently, a natural resource has become a legal subject resulting in the common public spending schemes and projects from the Central and State governments for maintenance, desalination and reconstruction of tanks, ponds *etc.*

"Water" is placed in the Constitution in Entry 17 of List II (State List) of Schedule VII. However, the caveat is Entry 56 of List I (Union List), which says, "Regulations and development of inter-state rivers and river valleys to the extent to which such regulation and development under the control of the Union is declared Parliament by law to be expedient in the public interest. "Unfortunately, the Centre has made little use of the powers vested in it vide Entry 56 of List I. The result is that by virtue of Article 246 read with Entry 17, List II, states have exclusive jurisdiction over waters that are located within their territories, including inter-state rivers and river valleys. It is arguably this status of water in the Constitution that constrains the highest in the executive and the judiciary, despite their pronouncements on and commitment to resolving the problem. It also makes a mockery of the National Water Policy that declares water a "prime natural resource, a basic human need and a precious national asset". It has also stopped the Centre from establishing allocation rules and clearly defined water rights among states that have unending disputes over the sharing of interstate water resources. The latest example is the second

Krishna Water Disputes Tribunal, which has turned into a warzone, with a battery of lawyers, technical staff and irrigation department officials from Maharashtra, Karnataka and Andhra Pradesh fighting to win the maximum allocation of the Krishna River for their respective state.

The Centre has also been reluctant to take a proactive position on the Convention on the Law of the Non-Navigational Uses of International Water-courses (CLNNUIW), a document adopted by the UN on May 21, 1997, pertaining to the use and conservation of all waters that cross international boundaries, including surface and ground water. Unfortunately, the convention is not yet ratified. Alongside the US, China, Canada and Australia, India is among the major opponents of the CLNNUIW. A ratification by nations to pressure China against the diversion of the Brahmaputra. Several Chinese projects in west-central Tibet may have a bearing on river water flow into India as well as Bangladesh. There are also reports that China is planning to divert 200 billion cubic metres (BCM) of the Brahmaputra from south to north to feed the Yellow River. If this is true, India will face a severe crisis once the Chniese projects are completed. Many of the hydel projects in the Northeast may have to be shelved. Of the 1,900 BCM is generated in the Brahmaputra, one can imagine what would happen if the bulk of this is diverted by China. According to a recent World Bank report, entitled "India's Water Economy: Bracing for a Turbulent Future", "faced with poor water supply services, farmers and urban dwellers alike have resorted to helping themselves by pumping out ground water through tube-wells... it has led to rapidly declining water tables and critically depleted aquifers, and is no longer sustainable(at many places)." The report adds that "government actions-including the provision of highly subsidized or even free power have exacerbated rather than addressrd the problem."

India is getting seriously water-stressed; and we need to act fast. Water has to be treated not as a local resource, but a global resource. We need to see if a change in its constitutional status is required. Similarly, we need to proactively decide on our stand on the proposed UN convention.

The inherited art of water harvesting has been conveniently forgotten by people. After the state became the absolute owner, the involvement of its citizens in safeguarding them was given up and community involvement drastically diminished. Today water governance is suffering from institutional paralysis at the hands of unaware and inattentive users.

The lack of awareness of water sources leads to a tragedy of converting water bodies into land areas. In a case before the Madras High Court, (W.P. (MD) No. 2779/07 dt. 1ih November 2007 Dr. R.S. Lal Mohan Vs Executive engineer, WRO), the shrinking of water sources was brought to the notice of the judiciary, by a pro bono public petition. The court expressed its anguish over the disappearance of tanks. As per the census taken in 1962, in Kanyakumari district of Tamil Nadu, more than 3,500 waterbodies were noticed and identified, but in 1998 more than 1,000 of these tanks were lost.

The arbitrary use of waterbodies for various other purposes by the state without considering the ecological consequences and the lack of reponse from the community are the main cause of groundwater depletion. Thus, the people who raise their voice for the right to water have to relies their own faults and failure to protect the natural water harvesting bodies.

Therefore, water-sensitisation is a prerequisite to claim-rights and entitlements. Creating awareness among and engaging local bodies and their representatives in the maintenance of water harvesting and storing structures is an important preliminary work to be undertaken by the state and non-governmental organizations.

Government of India provides technical and financial assistance to the State Governments for increasing storage as well as utilization of water for irrigation, domestic and industrial uses, etc. As per available information, storage capacity of about 263 billion cubic meter (BCM) has been created in the country so far. The total estimated storage capacity of the various projects under construction is about 51 BCM. Further, the State Governments have identified various other schemes for investigation and planning and the estimated storage for such schemes is about 110 BCM.

A writ Petition 724/1994 with the title "and Quiet Flows the Maily Yamuna" was filed in the Supreme Court during Sept. 2002 by Mr. Ranjit Kumar, Sr. Advocate (Amicus Curiae) quoting the speech of Hon'ble President of India dated 14th August 2002 where need for networking of Rivers had been mentioned and prayed for appropriate directions. The Supreme Court directed to treat this issue as an independent Public Interest Litigation (PIL) Writ Petition (Civil) NO.512 of 2002 with cause title: "Networking of rivers" and directed center and states to respond. In the mater of above PIL on 31st October, 2002 the Court made the following order:

Pursuant to the notice issued by this Court to all the States and the Union territories in relation to the inter-linking of the rivers and affidavit has been filed by the Union of India and also by the State of Tamil Nadu. No other State or Union Territory has filed any affidavit and the presumption, therefore, clearly is that they do not oppose the prayer made in this writ petition and it must be regarded that there is a consensus amongst all of them that there should be inter-linking of rivers in India.

In the counter affidavit filed on behalf of the Union of India, it has, interalia, been stated that after Rao Committee's Report was received, the Government of India has been studying and planning for inter-linking of rivers for over two decades. It is also mentioned in this affidavit that the Ministry of Water Resources had made a representation on 5th October, 2002 before the Prime Minister on inter-linking of rivers and in that presentation the Deputy Prime minister and other senior Ministers and officers were also present. It was suggested that a High Level Task Force can be formed which will go into the modalities for bringing consensus among the States. This affidavit further states that the presentation was also made to the President of India on 16th October, 2002 which also shows interest of the President of India in this project and it is in view of his broadcast to the nation on the eve of the Independence Day where emphasis was laid on inter-linking of rivers that has given rise to the filling of the present petition.

The Attorney General states that a High Powered Task Force, as referred in the Affidavit of the Union of India, has not yet been formed and by the next date of hearing he should be in a position to inform this Court with regard to the formation of the said task force as well as the decision of the said Force. The Union of India has accepted the concept of inter-linking of rivers and in the affidavit spelt out the benefits which will annure the entire project has been completed.

The State of Tamil Nadu is the only State which has responded to the notice issued by this Court and filed an affidavit. The said State also supports inter-linking of rivers and in its affidavit has prayed that a direction be issued to the Union of India for constituting a High Powered Committee in order to see that the project is completed in time schedule. Along with affidavit the prospective plan for implementation of inter-basin water transfer proposals prepared by the National Water Development Agency in May, 2000 has been placed on record. We are distressed to note that milestone for the perspective plan indicated in the report of the Agency shows that even though the Pre-Feasibility Reports regarding the Peninsular & Himalayan projects arc already completed, the completion of the link projects ultimately will be by the year 2035 in respect of Peninsular Link Project and 2003 regarding Himalayan Link Project.

The Attorney General states that a more realistic view will be taken and a revised programme on completion would draw up and be presented to the Court. We do expect that the programme when drawn up would try and ensure that the link projects are completed within a reasonable time of not more than ten years. We say so because recently the National Highways Projects have been undertaken and the same is nearing completion and the inter-linking of the rivers is complimentary to the state highway and the water ways which are constructed will be of immense benefit to the country as a whole.

The report of the National Water Development Agency refers to negotiations and signing of agreements. This aspect is also adverted to by the Union of India in its affidavit when it mentioned that consent of all the States affected by the Inter-linking of these, rivers has to be obtained. Learned Attorney General would like to consider this aspect as it is contended by Mr. Ranjit Kumar that if a legislation under Entry 56 list I of the Constitution is made, the need for the consent would not arise and the Centre would be in a position to undertake the project and complete the same within a reasonable period of time.

It is not open to this Court to .issue any direction to the Parliament to legislate but the Attorney General submits that the Government will consider this aspect and, if so advised, will bring an appropriate legislation.

Mr. Ranjit Kumar, learned amicus has drawn our attention to River Board Act, 1956 which has been enacted by the Parliament. Learned Attorney General would look into this in order to examine whether any further piece of legislation is necessary for bringing about the inter-linking of the rivers.

The parties are at liberty to file in Court any reports or papers containing studies in respect of the said, project. To come up for further orders on 16th December, 2002.

Upon hearing the counsel on 16th December, 2002 the Court made the following order:

"Learned Attorney General has brought to our notice resolution dated 13.12.2002 passed by Ministry of Water Resources, Government of India, inter alia, stating that National Water Development Agency has, after carrying out detailed studies and investigations for preparation of feasibility reports identified 30 links and prepared feasibility r.eports of six. such links. It also notices that various basin States have expressed divergent views about the studies and feasibility reports prepared by the said Agency and with a view to bringing out a consensus among the States and provide guidance on norms of appraisal of individual projects and modalities for project funding etc. the Central Government has set up a Task Force details whereof are given in paras 3 & 4 of the resolution. Para 5 sets out the terms of reference of the said Task Force and para 8 sets out the time table for achieving the goal of inter-linking of rivers by the end of 2016. Mr. Ranjit Kumar, learned amicus curiae, prays for a short adjournment for filing response thereto. List on 20th January, 2003."

Upon hearing counsel on 20th January, 2003 Court made the following order: "It would be expedient if the matter is adjourned by about three months so that the Court is in a position to know as to what progress has been made in the matter. List the matter in the 1st weeks of May, 2003."

Upon hearing the case on 5th May, 2003, the Hon'ble Supreme Court made the following order:

Pursuant to order dated 20th January, 2003, an affidavit dated 5th May, 2003 ahs been filed by Mr. B.P. Pandey, Deputy Commissioner, Ministry of Water Resources, Government of India, annexing thereto the resolution dated 13.12.2002 constituting a Task Force, time table for inter-linking of rivers, other resolutions nominating part time and full time members of the Task Force and few other documents. it seems that in last about four months three meetings of Task Force have been held on 6th January, 2003 27th March, 2003 and 28th April, 2003. In the last meeting the first Action Plan as per Government Resolution was considered and adopted. Now as per Action Plan-I the schedule for implementation is 10 years from the start. It stipulates that the work on the links can be started from 2007. It is envisaged to be completed by say end of 2016. Further it envisages that the group of Task Force of interlinking rivers will examine the two schedules and is expected to arrive at a reasonable and predicable implementation schedule in due course. According to action Plan-I the said Task Force has laid emphasis on demonstrative value of starting work on a link or two, as soon as possible. The process of preparation of Detailed Project Report for an inter basin link need to cover also, Detailed environmental Impact Assessment, Environmental Management Plan and R&R Plan for project affected persons. We find no substance in the apprehension that the Task Force will not implement the law. We have also no doubt that in case the other experts in the field provide necessary inputs to the Task Force, it will give due consideration the same deserves. For the present, we would direct posting of the matter after six months.

Upon hearing the case on 10th Nov, 2003 the Hon'ble Supreme Court made the following order:

Union of India is directed to file an affidavit placing on record up-to-date progress in the matter within a period of six weeks. List the matters thereafter.

Upon hearing the case on 6th Jan, 2004 the Hon'ble Supreme Court made the following order:–

- The Task Force of Interlinking of Rivers has filed a Progress Report, which deals with various aspects. It, inter alia, mentions that Interlinking of rivers have two major components i.e. Himalayan Component (14 links) and Peninsular component (16 links) It. further ment!ons that the former component i.e. Himalayan links requires an understanding with neighboring countries like Bhutan and Nepal. We hope that steps are being taken to have requisite discussions with the said countries. Regarding Peninsular link, the progress report records that in respect of two Iinks-(1) Ken-Betwa link (U.P. and M.P.) and (2) Parbati-Kalisindh-Chambal link (M.P. and Rajasthan), quick implementation is feasible in respect of the first link. In respect of the first link, feasibility Report is stated to be complete and Central Water Commission has been asked to initiate steps for preparation of Detailed Project Report. It is, however, not indicated as to when the said DPR is likely to be prepared. In respect of Second, the Report notes that National Water Development Agency has been directed to take necessary steps to" prepare Feasibility Report by March, 2004 so as to take action for preparation of DPR thereafter. It is stated by learned counsel appearing for Union of India that in respect of these two links the State of Madhya Pradesh and State of Rajasthan have given their consent and the discussions with State of Uttar Pradesh are at advance stage and the Feasibility Report may be filed by Union of India by 23rd April, 2004 and the matter shall be listed in the last week of April, 2004.

Upon hearing the case on 26th April 2004, the Hon'ble Supreme Court made the following order:–

- Pursuant to the order dated 6th January, 2004, an affidavit by Joint Commissioner (Basin Management), Ministry of.Watp.r Resources, Government of India, dated 23rd April, 2004, has been filed. We have perused the said affidavit of which details the progress in the matter of interlinking of rivers. Dealing with the follow up action on signing of the Memorandum of Understanding (MOU) between Madhya Pradesh and Uttar Pradesh and between Madhya Pradesh and Rajasthan, the affidavit states that the Government of Madhya Pradesh has communicated its consent to sign the MOU while the matter is under discussion with the Governments of Rajasthan and Uttar Pradesh and efforts are being made to sort out the differences. With regard to the follow up action by Central Water Commission and National Water Development Agency, it has been stated that the detailed project report for Ken-Betwa link is proposed be completed by Central Water Commission in thirty months. Our attention as drawn to the time table for interlinking of rivers already filed, according to which, for completion of detailed project report, the time stipulated was 31st December, 2006. The feasibility report of Parbati-Kalisindh-Chamballink is stated to have been completed in March, 2004.

In respect of putting the feasibility report on website, an affidavit be filed along with the next progress report. Prima facie we cannot contemplate any reason for the feasibility report not putting on website. In the affidavit to be filed, the aspect of central Legislation, as noticed in this Court's order dated 31st October, 2002, be also indicated.

Further progress report and the affidavit shall be filed within four months.

Upon hearing the case on 30th August, 2004 the Hon'ble Supreme Court made the following order:–

• We have perused the affidavit of Mr. M.S. Gupta, Senior Joint Commissioner (Basin Division), Ministry of Water Resources; Government of India dated 24th August, 2004 along with which progress report in the matter of interlinking of rivers has been filed. The progress report being not very clear on our query learned Solicitor General States that the Government has taken, in principal, decision to continue with interlinking of rivers. The mater, after comprehensive review is likely to be placed before the Cabinet after about six weeks. The report of the Standing Committee on Water resources has been taken on record. Our attention has also been drawn By Mr. Ranjit Kumar, Amicus to the Report of the Standing Committee on Water Resources 2004-2005 inter alia stating that the committee desires that the Government to make earnest efforts to get going the interlinking of the Northern and Southern rivers under ILR Programme in a definite time schedule which, in their considered view, would save the nation from the devastating ravages of chronic droughts and follows. Be that as it may, as prayed by learned Solicitor General, we defer the matter by eight weeks. The up-to date progress report is filed within eight weeks and the matter be listed thereafter. Upon hearing the case on 1 st November, 2004, the Hon'ble Supreme Court made the following order:–

• Pursuant to orders dated 30th August, 2004, a progress report in the matter of "Interlinking of rivers" has been filed in the form of an annexure (Ar:mexure R-9) to the affidavit of Shri M.S. Gupta, Senior Joint Commissioner (Basin Management), Ministry of Water Resources. Learned Solicitor General has also brought to our notice the presentation on the aspect of interlinking of rivers which was made by the Ministry of Water resources in a high powered meeting, comprising of the Prime Minister, Union Minister of Finance, Deputy Chairman, Planning Commission,

Member, Planning Commission, and Member Secretary to the Prime Minister amongst others. That presentation was made on 11th October, 2004. With reference to the project reports pertaining to link between Ken-Betwa which has a length of 231 Kms. and the link between Parbati-Kalisindh-Chambal with a length of 243 Kms., in the first link there being two States (U.P. & M. P.) and in the second link again there being two States (M.P. & Rajasthan), it has been, inter alia, stated that the consensus group has been asked to intensify its efforts with a view to resolve technical issue with that State Governments and submit its report by November, 2004. The presentation, however, stipulates that after the receipt of the report that may be submitted November 2004, the Secretary (Water Resources) will hold discussions with concerned State Governments followed by Political level meetings to reach an understanding so that preparation of Detailed Project Reports (DPRs) can start. It has also been stipulated that other apprehensions of States will be addressed at DPR stage. The presentation has prioritized the different project components for preparation of DPRs and implementation.

In regard to involvement of environmentalists and others, this Court in its order dated 5th May, 2003 had directed that the process of preparation of DPRs for an inter basin link needs to cover also a detailed environmental impact assessment, environmental management plan and R&R plan for project affected persons. An apprehension was expressed at that stage that the matters of environment may be over looked in the implementation of this project. This Court found no substance in the apprehension that the Task Force would not implement the law. It was observed that in case other experts in the field provide necessary inputs, that would be given due consideration it deserves. Now, a perusal of the present port shows that it has been specifically noticed that a group of environmentalists, social activists and other experts will be constituted by the Ministry of Water Resources which will be involved in the consultative process for the project. In the order dated 26th, April, 2004, we had observed that, Prima facie, it is not possible to contemplate any reason for the feasibility report not being put on website. In the Status Report, it has been mentioned that the Chairman, Governing Body, NWDA and Secretary (Water Resources) has directed NWDA on 13th October, 2004 to take further action for putting the feasibility report on Ken-Betwa Link on website. For further, consideration the matter shall be placed before the Court in the last week of January of first week of February, 2005.

Upon hearing the case on 4th Feb. 2005 the Hon'ble Supreme Court made the following order:–

- The learned counsel for the Union of India prays for four weeks' time to file the status report. Prayer is allowed and the writ petitions are adjourned.

UPON hearing counsel the Court made the following ORDER on 8th April, 2005: We have perused the status report filed in the form of an affidavit of Shri M.S. Gupta, Senior Joint Commissioner (Basin Management), Ministry of Water Resources, Government of India.

In so far as Ken-Betwa link is concerned, though, the affidavit and the documents accompanying it state that the Principal Secretary, Government of Uttar Pradesh, would inform the decision of the Government by the end of January, 2005, we are told by the learned Solicitor General that the Government of Uttar Pradesh has conveyed its consent, subject to certain conditions, in particular the condition of funding. The cost of preparation of the Detailed Project Report {for short, "D. P.R."} is proposed to be done from Central funding amounting to Rupees thirty crores. We take note of the fact that now a Memorandum of Understanding is required to be signed between the Government of Uttar Pradesh and the Central Government

In so far as Parbati-Kalisindh-Chambal link is concerned, the consensus group headed by the Chairman, Central 'Water Commission, held its meeting on 2nd November, 2004, and discussed the issues raised by the Governments of Rajasthan and Madhya Pradesh regarding Parbati-Kalsindh-Chambal link. The group submitted its report to the Ministry. The Governments of Rajasthan and Madhya Pradesh were asked to give concurrence for signing the Memorandum of Understanding so that the work for preparation of D.P.R. could commence. It seems that certain issues are still to be sorted out with the State of Rajasthan even after inter-State meeting of Chief Secretaries held on 11th January, 2005. We hope that the issues would be sorted out without the intervention of the Court.

The Office Memorandum dated 29th December, 2004 shows that the task force on inter-linking of rivers, having submitted its report, has been wound up with effect from 31st December, 2004 and a special cell is constituted to look after the residuary work of the task force and for taking follow up action on the inter-linking of river programmes under the Ministry of Water Resources. That special cell was earlier headed by a Joint Secretary but not in terms of Office memorandum dated 15th February, 2005, it has been directed to be headed by the Commissioner (Project) in the said Ministry.

It may also be noted that the terms of reference of the Environmentalists Committee, above noted, seem to be quite comprehensive and that is the reason we have directed that all concerned may place their view-point before the said Committee. The next status report is filed within three months.

UPON hearing counsel the Court made the following Order on 8th August, 2005: Contempt Petition (c) NO.163 of 2005:

- The grievance made in this petition. is that, despise repeated orders of this Court, the respondents have not put the feasibility reports on website, except the feasibility report in respect of Ken-Betwa Link project. The orders that have been passed this Court for putting the feasibility reports on website are dated 26th April, 2004, 1 st November, 2004 and 8th April, 2005. The advantage of putting the said reports on website has also been indicated in the order dated 8th April, 2005. With reference to the orders earlier passed, it was directed on 8th April, 2005, that feasibility reports shall be put on website soon after its completion. Pursuant to the order dated 8th April, 2005, Mr. K. Vohra, Senior Joint Commissioner (Basin Management), Ministry of Water Resources, had filed a status report in the form of an affidavit in respect of some of the links. It is stated that the Government of Gujarat has not agreed to put feasibility report on the website and the response of other concerned State, namely, Maharashtra, is awaited. This is in respect of Par-Tapi Narmada and Damanganga-Pinjal links. We fail to understand, where was the necessity for the Government of India to ask any other authority or State Government for its agreement for placing the feasibility reports on website when specific orders have been passed by this Court. If Government of India or any State had any difficulty in implementing the direction of placing the feasibility reports on website, it was open to them to approach this Court and seek further directions. Nothing of the kind has been done by any of the parties or the Government.

Mr. Goolam E. Vahanvati, Solicitor General, states that it appears that the feasibility report of Parbati Kalisindh-Chambal Link project has also been put on website recently.

At present, though we are not inclined to take any action as sought for in this contempt petition in view of the submission of the learned Solicitor General that there was some confusion in the mind of some 0fficers in respect of the direction made for putting the feasibility reports on website, we direct that all such feasibility reports, which are ready and complete, shall be put on website without reference to any person or authority and without any further delay. This would dispose of the contempt petition.

In respect of Parbati Kalisindh-Chambal link, the affidavit shows that the matter h.as already been discussed at the level of Consensus Building Group. It is pointed out that the Chief Ministers of the States of Rajasthan and Madhya Pradesh are expected to meet shortly and discuss various issues. In respect of Ken-Betwa link, from the affidavit, it appears that though the Government of Madhya Pradesh has given its consent, the Government of Uttar Pradesh has not even responded. Reference in' this affidavit has been made to the letter written on 19th, 2005. It is stated that the response from the State of Uttar Pradesh is still awaited. The learned counsel for the State of Uttar Pradesh is present but without any instructions. We direct the State of Uttar Pradesh to cooperate in the matter. For the present, we say no more. Further, it has been brought to our notice by the learned Solicitor General that papers for convening the meeting of the committee of Environmentalists, Social Scientists and other experts have been processed and it is expected that a date for the said meeting will be fixed shortly of which sufficient notice would be given to Mr. Ranjit Kumar, learned Amicus Curiae.

In respect of Godavari (Polavaram)-Krishna (Vijayawada) Link, Damanganga-Pinjal Link and Par-Tapi Narmada Link, it has been stated in the affidavit that sixth meeting of Consensus Group is stated to be now fixed for 23rd August, 2005.

SUPREME COURT DISMISSES PLEA TO REVIEW

Central Ground Water Authority had said the Order Could Amount to Judicial Overreach

The Supreme Court had dismissed a petition seeking a review of its order, directing the Central and stare governments to expedite the controversial project to interlink rivers to transfer water from water surplus areas to water deficit regions. The review petition was filed by the Central Ground Water Authority (CGWA) and said that the court order [1] dated February 27 could be interpreted as judicial overreach.

At the same time, the apex court bench of Chief Justice S H Kapadia, Justice Swatanter Kumar and justice A K Patnaik refused permission for filling of a similar review petition by 21 eminent citizens. The bench, in its order on September 26, 2012 said both petitions were delayed and lacked merit.

The two petitions raised concerns over impacts of interlinking of rivers. The eminent citizens who have questioned the project include former secretary of water resources, Ramaswamy R Iyer and social activist Medha Patkar.

On February 27, the court had asked the Central and state governments to expedite the necessary feasibilitv reports and detailed proiect reports for the 30 links that would connect various rivers [1]. The judgement upheld the importance of interlinking of rivers in view of the paradoxical situation wherein floods and droughts occur at almost the same time in different parts of the country.

Some States Oppose River Interlinking

Most states have agreed to cooperate with Central government to expedite the projects but the problems arising from them, like rehabilitaton and resettlement of the people to be displaced, are yet to be resolved.

The National Advisory Council was entrusted with making the draft national policy on resettlement and rehabilitation.

Some states like Kerala and Karnataka have, however, have opposed the projects. Karnataka is yet to grant permission for the Bedti-Varada and Netravati Hemavati-Tapi links. The state government even opposed feasibility study of these river links due to cases relating to water sharing pending in other courts. This was noted by the apex court in its February order.

Kerala has staunchly opposed the long distance interbasin transfer of river water in the state, saying the state needs water to maintain its intricate network of natural and man made channels and supply water for irrigation and drinking.

The Supreme Court in its judgement had observed the state's hesitation in implementing the project because it experiences severe water scarcity during summer and off monsoon months. The court had earlier noted that even states like Uttar Pradesh have not granted comprehensive approvals for projects such as the Ken-Betwa link

The February judgement, however, allows the amicus curiae Ranjith Kumar to file a contempt plea if the orders of the court are violated by either the states or the Central government. The court has also appointed a committee, comprising experts from Ministry of Water Resources, Ministry of Agriculture, Ministry of Environment and Forests, social activists and others to speedily execute the project.

J.M.V. Kamath said on Interlinking of Rivers on 02 February 2012, the Supreme Court directed the Union Government to implement the ambitious River Inter-linking Project (RIP) in a time-hound manner and appointed a high-powered committee for its planning and completion. Inevitably, it evoked an outcry against the very concept from important segments of the public. It is not that the Supreme Court was stepping beyond its prescribed duties. In its ruling the Supreme Court conceded that it is not epuipped to take such decisions "which essentially should be left for the Central Government and the concerned state".

The verdict further said that "this Court may not be very appropriate for planning and implantation of such a programme, having wide national dimensions and ramifications" The Court also acknowledged that "some Indian states are opposed to the project and showed' its awareness of possible "development induced displacement and the "cost of resettlement of displaced people" .

A more rational explanation is that in state where landlessness is high, a large number of small and marginal farmers would face pauperization, inflate migration and crowd the footpaths of major townships in the country.

According to a study reported in Economic and Political Weekly (21 April), of 54 large dams, the number of people displaced by one dam is 44.182. The study conducted by the Indian Institute of Public Administration showed that in thelast 50 years, as many as 33 million had been displaced. Apart from that, many are of the opinion that just the cost of implementing the RIP should make the government wary of taking up the assignment.

As of now, it is claimed, the cost could go up by more than ten times the earlier figures. Would that be balanced by the advantages that would accrue in linking 30 major peninsular rivers? One advantage, it is claimed, it that the Project would help generate 40,000 MW of "clean and green energy". Another is that "we can bring in nine crore acres of additional wet lands into farming, benefitting 45 crore people.

The normal annual Indian surface water resources are about 68,969. Thousand Million Cubic feet (TMC) of'which only 8,814 TMC or 13 per cent is used. We have all the water we need. What we additionally need is care and concern to see that good intentions do not end up as social disasters. We can do without the latter. The one practical step we can take is not to insist on 'time-bound' execution of RIP.

INTER-LINKING RIVERS RECIPE FOR DISASTER

The ecological, economic and social costs of interlinking rivers are going to be enormous. You would be shocked if someone told you that the apex court has recently directed the central government to redefine the geography of India. This made no 'breaking news' on television but this is exactly what the court had directed.

Once all the rivers are linked up as part of this grand design, then the map of India would certainly look different and we will have to change Indian maps in all our geography text books, It is this plan of reengineering India's geography that the court has put its seal on and wants the government to implement because, in its opinion, it is in 'national interest'.

The ecological, economic and social costs of interlinking rivers are going to be enormous. All these concerns were articulated during the public debate that took place when the NDA government wanted to push this project as a 'nationalist' dream a decade ago.

The interlinking would involve about 30 large projects and construction of 80 dams all over the country. Just imagine the ecological devastation it would cause in different parts of the country. There is no estimation as yet of how much it would cost, but one can say it certainly has all ingredients of giving rise to a million scams.

When you say a river is 'surplus' you are ignoring multiple purposes that it serves as it flows through different regions before joining the sea. Similarly the concept of a 'deficit' river is largely based on 'demands' on its waters due to wasteful uses. The group has suggested a rational approach-careful, economical, conflict-free and sustainable intra-basin management rather than inter-basin transfers. This is very important, given the fact that river water disputes between states as well as with neighbouring countries are already a political problem. Some states have expressed their concerns over interlinking project ignore all such ground realities.

'River are not pipelines'–the group says while arguing against creation of a national water grid. Any rationally thinking person would fully endorse this view because rivers are lifelines. They support the whole ecosystem. They are not mere carriers of water. Hope Me Lordships will see the rationale.

●●●

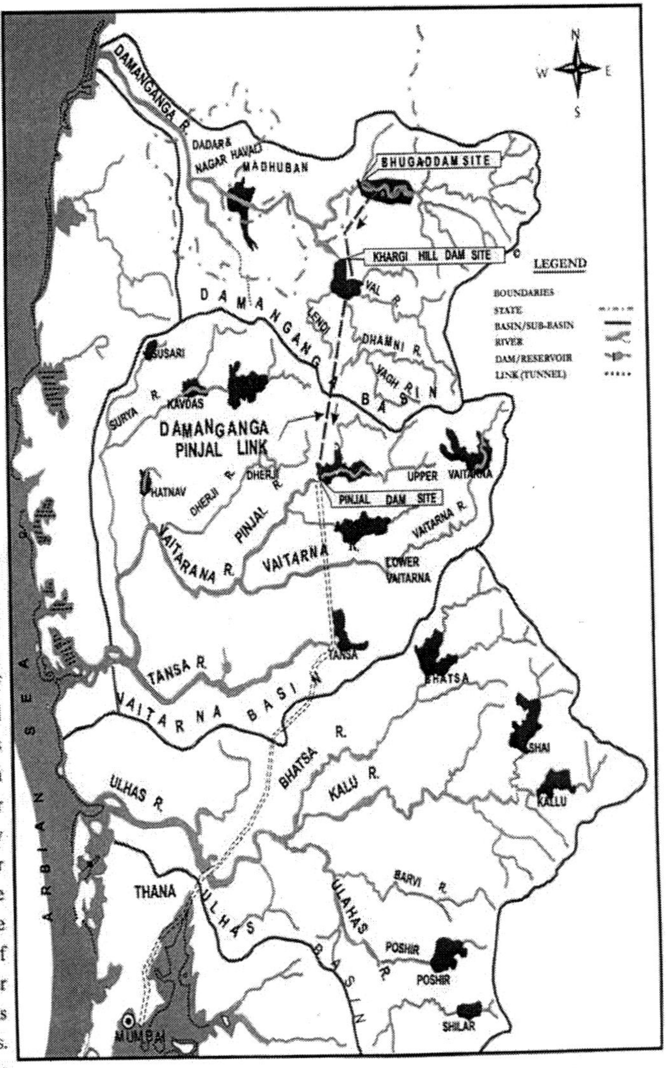

Present status of the link projects

On receiving the concurrence from the concerned State Govts. of Maharashtra and Gujarat, NWDA has taken up preparation of the Detailed Project Reports of both Par-Tapi-Narmada & Damanganga-Pinjal during January, 2009. Subsequently, on 3rd May, 2010 a Memorandum of Understanding has been signed in this regard by Hon'ble Chief Ministers of Gujarat and Maharashtra States with Hon'ble Union Minister for Parliamentary Affairs and Water Resources in the presence of Hon'ble Prime Minister of India. The work for preparation of DPRs is under progress. NWDA plans to accomplish the entrusted tasks of preparing the DPRs by using latest available data in a fully consultative manner considering the views and demands of local people/stakeholders.

Courtsey—NWDA, Govt. of India

Appendix-I

Annexure

No. 2/21/2002-BM

GOVERNMENT OF INDIA

MINISTRY OF WATER RESOURCES

New Delhi, the 13th December, 2002

Resolution

The Ministry of Water Resources (then known as Ministry of Irrigation) in the year 1980 formulated a National Perspective Plan for water resources development by transferring water from water surplus basins to water deficit basins/regions by inter-linking of rivers. The National Perspective Plan has two main components i.e. the Himalayan Water Development Agency (NWDA) was set up as a Society under the Societies Registration Act, 1860 in 1982 to carry out the detailed studies and detailed surveys and investigations and to prepare feasibility reports of the links under the National Perspective Plan.

2. NWDA has, after carrying out detailed studies, identified 30 links for preparation of feasibility reports and has prepared feasibility reports of 60 such links. The various basin States have expressed divergent views about the studies and feasibility reports prepared by NWDA. With a view to bringing about a consensus among the States and provide guidance on norms of appraisal of individual projects and modalities for project funding etc. the Central Government hereby sets up a Task Force.

3. The Task Force shall be as under:

(i) Shri Suresh Prabhu, Member of Parliament, Lok Sabha, Chairman

(ii) Shri C.C. Patel, Vice-Chairman; and

(iii) Dr. C.D. Thatte, Member-Secretary.

4. In addition to the above members of the Task Force, part-time members will also be nominated in consultation with the Chairman of the Task Force and with the approval of the Prime Minister. These part-time members will be as under:

(i) A member from water deficit States

(ii) A person from water surplus States

(iii) An economist

(iv) A sociologist; and

(v) A legal/world wild life expert.

5. The terms of reference of the Task Force will be to:

(i) Provide guidance on norms of appraisal of individual projects in respect of economic viability, socio-economic impacts, environmental impacts and preparation of resettlement plans;

(ii) Devise suitable mechanism for bringing about speedy consensus amongst the States;

(iii) Prioritize the different project components for preparation of Detailed Project Reports and implementation;

(iv) Propose suitable organizational structure for implementing the project;

(v) Consider various modalities for projects funding; and

(vi) Consider international dimensions that may be involved in some project components.

6. The Task Force shall have its headquarters in New Delhi and shall meet as and when necessary.

7. The terms and conditions for Chairman, Vice-Chairman, Member-Secretary and other Members shall be decided in due course.

8. The milestone/time table for achieving the goal of inter-linking of rivers by the end of 2016.

9. The Financial provisions of the Task Force will be regulated as under:

(i) All the capital and revenue expenditure required to be incurred by the Task Force shall be borne by the Central Government through the grants-in-aid to National Water Development Agency; and

(ii) National Water Development Agency will account for expenditure of the Task Force as a part of its establishment expenditure and would provide such other secretarial/ministerial assistance as may be required. Audit of Controller General of Accounts and Comptroller and Auditor General of India would be incident on such expenditure in the same manner as it would be on National Water Development Agency's other usual expenditure.

Sd/-

VIJAY KUMAR

Deputy Secretary to the Government of India

(i)	Notification of the Task Force	By 16-12-2002
(ii)	Preparation of Action Plan-I, giving as 30-04-2003 outline of the time schedules for the completion of the feasibility studies, detailed project reports, estimated cost. Implementation schedule, concrete benefits and advantages of the project, etc.	
(iii)	Preparation of Action Plan-II, giving alternative options for funding and	31-07-2003

	execution of the project as also the suggested methods for cost recovery.	
(iv)	Meeting with the Chief Ministers to delibrate over the project and to elicit their cooperation.	May/June, 2003 to deliberate
(v)	Completion of Feasibility Studies (already in progress).	31-12-2005
(vi)	Completion of Detailed Project Reports. (Preparation of DPRs will start simultaneously) since FSs in respect of six river links have already been completed).	31-12-2006
(vii)	Implementation of the Project (10 years).	31-12-2006

Appendix-II

National Environment Policy–2004

1. Preamble

A diverse developing society such as ours provides numerous challenges in the economic, social, political, cultural and environmental arenas. All of these coalesce in the dominant imperative of alleviation of mass povery, reckoned in the multiple dimensions of livelihood security, health care, education, empowerment of the disadvan-taged and elimination of gender disparities.

The present national policies for environmental management are contained in the National Forest Policy 1988, the National Conservation Strategy and Policy State-ment on Environment and Development, 1992; and a Policy Statement on Abatement of Pollution. 1992. Some sector policies such as the National Water Policy, 2002 have also contributed towards environmental management. Despite these policy documents a need for a comprehen-sive policy statement has been evident for some time in order to infuse a common approach to the various sectoral, cross-sectoral, including fiscal, approaches to environ-mental management. As our development challenges have evolves and our understanding of the centrality of environmental concerns in development has sharpened, there is also a need to review the earlier objectives, policy instruments, and strategies.

This dynamic requires an evolving and flexible policy framework with a built in system for monitoring and review, and where necessary, revision. Sustainable development concerns in the sense of enhancement of human well-being, broadly conceived, are a recurring theme in India's development philosophy. For this to occur, there is a need for balance and harmony between economic, social and environmental needs of the country. India also plays an important role in several significant international initiatives concerned with the environment. It is a party to the key multilateral agreements, and reco-gnizes the interdependency among, and transboundary character of, several environmental problems.

The National Environment Policy (NEP, 2004) is a response to our national commitment to a clean environment, mandated in the Constitution in Articles 48A and 51A (g), strengthened by judicial interpretation of Article 21. It is recognized that maintaining a healthy environment is not the state's responsibility alone, but also that of every citizen. A spirit of partnership should thus be realized throughout the spectrum of environmental management in the country. While the state must galvanise its efforts, there should also be recognition by each individual–natural or institutional, of its responsibility towards main-taining and enhancing the quality of the environment. The NEP, 2004 is also intended to be a statement of India's commitment to making a positive contribution to interna-tional efforts.

The NEP, 2004 is intended to be a guide to action: in regulatory reform, programmes and projects for environmental conservation; and review and enactment of legislation, by agencies of the Central, State and Local Governments. It also seeks to stimulate partnerships of different stakeholder, i.e. public agencies, local communities, the investment community, and interna-tional development partners, in harnessing their respective resources and strengths for environmental management. On the whole, it is expected to do better than fiscal neutrality, and likely raise substantial resources from outside the fiscal regime to realize its objectives.

2. Key Environmental Challenges: Causes and Impacts

The key environmental challenges that the country faces relate to the nexus of environmental degradation with poverty in its many dimensions, and economic growth. These challenges are intrinsically connected with the state of environmental resources, such as land, water, air and their flora and fauna. The proximate drivers of environmental degradation are population growth, technology and consumption choices, and poverty, leading to changes in relations between people and ecosystems, and development activities such as intensive agriculture, polluting industry, and unplanned urbanization. However, these factors give rise to environ-mental degradation only through deeper causal linkages, in particular institutional failures, resulting in lack of clarity or enforcement of rights of access and use of environ-mental resources, policies which provide disincentives for environmental conservation (and which may have origins in the fiscal regime), and governance constraints.

3. The Objectives of NEP 2004

The principal objectives of this policy are enumerated below. These objectives relate to current perceptions of key environmental challenges. They may, accordingly, evolve over time:

i. Conservation of Critical Environmental Resources

To protect and conserve critical ecological systems and resources, and invaluable natural and man-made heritage which are essential for life-support, livelihoods, economic growth, and a broad conception of human well-being.

ii. Inter-genrational Equity:Livelihood Security for the Poor

To ensure equitable access to environmental resources and quality for all sections of society, and in particular, to ensure that poor communities, which are most dependent on environmental resources for their livelihoods, are assured secure access to these resources.

iii. Inter-generational Equity

To ensure judicious use of environmental resources to meet the needs and aspirations of present and future generations.

iv. Integration of Environmental Concerns in Economic and Social Development

To integrate environmental concerns into policies, plans, programmes, and projects for economic and social development.

v. Efficiency in Environmental Resource Use

To ensure efficient use of environmental resources in the sense of reduction in their use per unit of economic output, to minimize adverse environmental impacts.

vi. Environmental Governance

To apply the principles of good governance (transparency, rationality, accountability, reduction in time and costs, and participation) to the management and regulation of use of environmental resources.

vii. Enhancement of Resources for Environmental Conser-vation

To ensure higher resource flows, comprising finance, technology, management skills, traditional knowledge, and social capital, for environmental conservation through mutually beneficial multistakeholder partnerships between local communities, public agencies, and investors.

Forests and Wildlife

Forests provide a multicity of environmental services. Foremost among these is the recharging of mountain aquifers, which sustain our rivers. They also conserve the soil, and prevent floods and drought. They provide habitat for wildlife and the ecological conditions for maintenance and natural evolution of genetic diversity of flora and fauna. They are the traditional homes of forest dwelling tribals, the major part by far of whose livelihoods depend on forests. They yield timber, fuel-wood, and other forest produce, and possess immense potential for economic benefits, in particular for local communities, from sustainable eco-tourism.

On the other hand, in recent decades, there has been significant loss of forest cover, although there are now tangible signs of reversal of this trend. The principal direct cause of forest loss has been the conversion of forests for agriculture, settlements, infrastructure, and industry. In addition, commercial extraction of fuel-wood, illegal felling, and grazing of cattle, has degraded forests. These causes, however, have their origins in the fact that the environmental values provided by forests are not realized as direct financial benefits by various parties, at least to the extent of exceeding the monetary incomes from alternative uses, including those arising from illegal use. Moreover, while since antiquity forest dwelling tribes had generally recognized traditional community rights over the forests, on account of which they had strong incentives to use the forests sustainably and to protect them from encroachers, following the commencement of formal forest laws and institutions in 1865, these rights were effectively extinguished in many parts of the country. Such disempowerment has led to the forests becoming open access in nature, leading to their gradual degradation in a classical manifestation of the "Tragedy of the Commons", besides leading to perennial conflict between the tribals and the Forest Department, and constituting a major denial of justice.

It is possible that some-specific non-forest activities may yield overall societal benefits significantly exceeding that from the environmental services provided by the particular tract of forest. However, large scale forest loss would lead to catastrophic, permanent change in the country's ecology, leading to major stress on water resources and soil erosion, with consequent loss of agricultural productivity, industrial potential, living conditions, and the onset of natural disasters including drought and floods. In any event, the environmental values of converted forests must be restored, as nearly as may be feasible, to the same publics.

Freshwater Resources

India's freshwater resources comprise the single most important class of natural endowments enabling its economy and its human settlement patterns. The freshwater resources comprise the river systems, ground water, and wetlands. Each of these has a unique role, and characteristic linkages to other environmental entities.

River Systems

India's river systems typically originate in its mountain eco-systems and deliver the major part of their water resources to the populations in the plains. They are subject to siltation from sediment loads due to soil loss, itself linked to loss of forest and tree cover. They are also subject to significant net water withdrawals along their course, due to agricultural, industrial, and municipal use; as well as pollution from human and animal waste, agricultural run-offs, and industrial effluents. Although the rivers possess significant natural capacity to assimilate and render harmless many pollutants, the existing pollutions inflows in most cases substantially exceed such natural capacities. This fact, together with progressive reductions in stream flows, ensures that the river water quality in the vast majority of cases declines as one goes downstream. The results include loss of aquatic flora and fauna, leading to loss of livelihoods for river fisherfolk, significant impacts on human health from polluted water, loss of habitat for many bird species, and loss of inland navigation potential. Apart from these, India's rivers are inextricably linked with the history and religious beliefs of its peoples, and the degradation of important river systems accordingly offends their spiritual, aesthetic, and cultural sensibilities.

The broad direct causes of rivers degradation are, in turn, linked to several policies and regulatory regimes. These include tariff policies for irrigation systems and industrial use, which, through inadequate cost-recovery, provide incentives overuse near the headwork's of irriga-tion systems, and drying up of irrigation systems at the tail-ends. The result is excessive cultivation of water inten-sive crops near the headwork's, which is otherwise ineffici-ent, waterlogging, and alkali-salinization of soil. The irriga-tion tariffs also do not yield resources for proper mainte-nance of irrigation systems, leading to loss in their poten-tial; in particular, resources are generally not available for lining irrigation canals to prevent seepage loss. These factors result in reduced flows in the rivers. Pollution loads are similarly linked to pricing policies leading to inefficient use of agricultural chemicals, and municipal and industrial water use. In particular, revenue yields for the latter two are insufficient to install and maintain sewage and effluent treatment plants, respectively. Pollution regulation for industries is typically not based on formal spatial planning to facilitate clustering of industries to realize scale economies in effluent treatment, resulting in relatively high costs of effluent treatment, and consequent increased incentives for non-compliance. There is, accordingly need to review the relevant pricing policy regimes and regulatory mechanisms in terms of their likely adverse environmental impacts.

The following comprise elements of an action plan for river systems:

(a) Promote integrated approaches to management of river basins by the concerned river authorities, considering upstream and downstream inflows and withdrawals by season, pollution loads and natural regeneration capacities, to ensure maintenance of adequate flows and adherence to water quality standards throughout course in all seasons.

(b) Consider and mitigate the impacts on river flora and fauna, and the resulting change in the resource base for livelihoods, of multipurpose river valley projects, power plants, and industries.

(c) Consider mandating the installation of water saving closets and taps in the building byelaws of urban centres.

Goundwater

Ground-water is present in underground aquifers in many parts of the country. Aquifers near the surface are subject to annual recharge from precipitation, but the rate of recharge in impacted by human interference. Deep aquifers, on the other hand, occur below a substratum of hard rock. The deep aquifers generally contain very pure water, but since they are recharged only over many millennia, must be conserved for use only in periods of calamitous drought such as may happen only once in several hundred years. The boundaries of ground-water aquifers do not generally correspond to the spatial jurisdiction of any local public authorities or private holdings, nor are they easily discernable, nor can withdrawals be easily monitored, leading to the unavoidable situation of ground-water being an open access resource.

The water table has been falling rapidly in many areas of the country in recent decades. This is largely due to withdrawal for agricultural, industrial, and urban use, in excess of annual recharge. In urban areas, apart from withdrawals for domestic and industrial use, housing and infrastructure such as roads, prevent sufficient recharge. In addition, some pollution of ground-water occurs due to leaching of stored hazardous waste and use of agricultural, in particular, pesticides. Contamination of ground-water is also due to geogenic causes, such as leaching of arsenic from natural deposits. Since ground-water is frequently a source of drinking water, its pollution leads to serious health impacts.

The direct causes of ground-water depletion have their origin in the pricing policies for electricity and diesel. In the case of electricity, where individual metering is not practiced, a flat charge for electricity connections makes the marginal cost of electricity effectively zero.

Subsidies for diesel also reduce the marginal cost of extraction to well below the efficient level. Given the fact that ground-water is an open access resource, the user then "rationally" (i.e. in terms of his individual perspective), extracts ground-water until the marginal value to him equals his now very low marginal cost of extraction. The result is inefficient withdrawals of ground-water by all users, leading to the situation of falling water tables. Support prices for several water intensive crops with implicit price subsidies aggravate this outcome by strengthening incentives to take up these crops rather than less water intensive ones.

Falling water tables have several perverse social impacts, apart from the likelihood of mining of deep aquifers, "the drinking water source of last resort". The capital costs of pump sets and bore wells for ground-water extraction when water tables are very deep may be relatively high, with no assurance that water would actually be found. In such a situation, a user who may be a marginal farmer able to borrow the money only at usurious rates of interest, may, in case water is not found, find it impossible to repay his debts. This may lead to destitution, or worse. Even if the impacts were not so dire, there would be excessive use of electricity and diesel.

The efficient use of ground-water would, accordingly, require that the practice of non-metering of electric supply to farmers be discontinued in their own enlightened self-interest. It would also be essential to progressively ensure that the environmental impacts are taken into account in setting electricity tariffs, and diesel pricing.

Increased run-off of precipitation in urban areas due to impermeable structures and infrastructure prevents ground-water recharge. This is an additional cause of falling water tables in urban areas. In rural areas several cost-effective contour bunding techniques have been proven to enhance ground-water recharge. A number of effective traditional water management techniques to recharge ground-water have been discontinued bye the local communities due to the onset of pump sets extraction, and need to be revived. Finally, increase in tree cover, is also effective in enhancing ground-water recharge.

Pollution of ground-water from agricultural chemicals is also linked to their improper use, once again due to pricing policies, especially for chemical pesticides, as well as agronomic practices, which do not take the potential environmental impacts into account. While transiting through soil layers may considerably eliminate organic pollution loads in ground-water, this is not true of several chemical pesticides.

The following action points emerge:

(a) Take explicit account of impacts on ground-water tables of electricity tariffs and pricing of diesel.

(b) Promote efficient water use techniques, such as sprinkler or drip irrigation, among farmers. Provide necessary pricing, inputs, and extension support to feasible and remunerative alternative crops from efficient water use.

(c) Support practices of contour bunding and revival

of traditional methods for enhancing ground-water recharge.

(d) Mandate water harvesting in all new construction in relevant urban areas, as well as design techniques for road surfaces and infrastructure to enhance ground-water recharge.

(e) Support R&D in cost effective techniques suita-ble for rural drinking water projects for removal of arsenic and mainstream their adoption in rural drinking water schemes in relevant areas.

Coastal Resources

Coastal environmental resources comprise a diverse set of natural and manmade assets, including mangroves, coral reefs, estuaries, coastal forests, genetic diversity, sand dunes, geomorphologies, sand beaches, land for agriculture and human settlements, coastal infrastructure, and heritage sites. These provide habitats for marine species, which, in turn comprise the resource base for large numbers of fisherfold, protection from extreme weather events, a resource base for sustainable tourism, and agricultural and urban livelihoods. In recent years there has been significant degradation of coastal resources, for which the proximate causes include poorly planned human settlements, improper location of industries, and infrastructure, pollution from industries and settlements, and overexploitation of living natural resources. In the future, sea level rise due to climate change may have major adverse impacts on the coastal environment. The deeper causes of these proximate factors lie in inadequate institutional capacities for, and participation of local communities in, formulation and implementation of coastal management plans, the open access nature of many coastal resources, and lack of consensus on means of provision of sanitation and waste treatment. The following further aspects may be addressed in an action plan:

(a) Mainstream the sustainable management of mangroves into the forestry sector regulatory regime, ensuring that they continue to provide livelihoods to local communities.

(b) Diseminate available techniques for regeneration of coral reefs, and support activities based on application of such techniques.

(c) Embody consideration of sea-level rise in coastal management plans, as well as infrastructure planning and construction norms.

Water Pollution

The Direct and indirect causes of pollution of surface (river, wetlands) water sources, ground-water, and coastal areas have been discussed above. The following coprise further elements of an action plan:

(a) Develop and implement, initially on a pilot scale, public-private partnership models for setting up and operating effluent and sewage treatment plants. Once the models are validated, progressi-vely use public resources including external assistance, to catalyze such partnerships. Enhance the capacities of municipalities for recovery of user charges for water and sewage systems.

(b) Enhance reuse of treated sewage and industrial waste-water before final discharge to water bodies.

(c) Enhance capacities for spatial planning among the State and local Governments, with adequate participation by local communities, to ensure clustering of polluting industries to facilitate setting up of common effluent treatment plants to be operated on cost recovery basis.

(d) Promote R&D in development of low cost technologies for sewage treatment at different scales, in particular, replication of the East Kolkata wetlands model for sewage treatment to yield multiple benefits.

(e) Take explicit account of ground-water pollution in pricing policies of agricultural inputs, especially pesticides, and dissemination of agronomy practices involving their use.

(f) Develop a strategy for strengthening regulation, and addressing impacts, of ship-breaking activities on coastal and near marine resources.

Review of the Policy

We live in a rapidly changing global community, in a rapidly developing, highly diverse country. The environmental issues that are salient as of now many enolve over time, and new onces may take their place. Scientific understanding of environmental matters would advance rapidly. Changes in economic structure, technologies, resource availability, in each case nationally as well as globally, are likely, as are evolution of global environ-mental regimes, and norms arising from jurisprudence.

To set forth an immutable National Environment Policy in this dynamic situation would be unwise. A prudent course would be to provide for updating every few years in light of new knowledge and developments, and a comprehensive review, perhaps overhaul, in about a decade.

The following provisions are, accordingly made for review, updating, and renewal of NEP 2004:

(a) Undertake consultation every three years with groups of diverse stakeholders, i.e. researchers and experts, community based organizations, industry association, and voluntary organizations, and update the National Environment Policy.

b) In the third of the three-year reviews, undertake a more comprehensive examination of the scientific and policy understanding of environ-mental issues, redefine the Objectives and Principles, and recast the Strategic Themes for Action. A new National Environment Policy should be the outcome.

Review of Implementation

Any policy is only as good as its implementation. The NEP, 2004 outlines a significant number of new and continuing initiatives for enhancing environmental conservation. These require the coordinated actions of diverse actors, for the major part organized and stimulated by one or more public agencies.

While coordination and review mechanisms are necessary in respect of the individual action plans under each of the strategic themes at relevant operational levels, a formal, periodic high level review of implementation of the different elements of NEP, 2004 is essential. This would enhance accountability of the different public agencies responsible for implementation. It would also reveal practical issues in implementation, including absence of political will at concerned levels, or official indifference.

Accordingly, the Cabinet Committee on Economic Affairs (CCEA) may be requested to review the implementation of NEP, 2004, once a year, within three months from the close of the previous fiscal year. The findings of the CCEA in the review should be publicly disclosed, so that stakeholders are assured of the serious-ness of the Government in ensuring implementation of the Policy.

Appendix-III

Government of India
Ministry of Water Resources
National Water Resources
Council Fifth Meeting

Vigyan Bhawan,
New Delhi.
Monday, the 1st April, 2002

Resolution

National Water Policy

The National Water Resources Council in its 2nd meeting held on 9th September, 1987 adopted the National Water Policy. This Policy has, since then, been guiding the formulation of policies and programmes for water resources development and its management. During last 14 years, many new challenges have emerged in the water resources sector which has necessitated the review of the existing National Water Policy.

Accordingly, the revised and updated draft National Water Policy, finalised by the Working Group, has been considered and deliberated upon in the 5th meeting of the National Water Resources Council held on 1st April, 2002. Some modifications have been suggested by the Members and also agreed to by the Council. In view of major consensus on the Policy, the Council resolves to adopt the (Revised) National Water Policy with modifications as agreed to by the Council and directs for its circulation to all concerned. The Policy would be titled as "National Water Policy-2002".

National Water Policy

National Water Policy was adopted in September, 1987. Since then, a number of issues and challenges have emerged in the development and management of the water resources.

Therefore, the National Water Policy (1987) has been reviewed and updated.

A well developed information system, for water related data in its entirety, at the national/state level, is a prime requisite for resource planning. A standardized national information system should be established with a network of data banks and data bases, integrating and strengthening the existing Central and State level agencies and improving the quality of data and the processing capabilities.

Standards for coding, classification, processing of data and methods/procedures for its collection should be adopted. Advances in information technology must be introduced to create a modern information system promi-ting free exchange of data among various agencies. Special efforts should be made to develop and continuously upgrade technological capability to collect, process and disseminate reliable data in the desired time frame.

Apart from the data regarding water availability and actual water use, the system should also include comprehensive and reliable projections of future demands of water for diverse purposes.

Water Resources Planning

Water resources available to the country should be brought within the category of utilizable resources to the maximum possible extent. Non-conventional methods for utilization of water such as through inter-basin transfers, artificial recharge of ground water and desalination of brackish or sea water as well as traditional water conservation practices like rainwater harvesting, including roof-top rainwater harvesting, need to be practiced to further increase the utilizable water resources. Promotion of frontier research and development, in a focused manner, for these techniques is necessary.

Water resources development and management will have to be planned for a hydrological unit such as drainage basin as a whole or for a sub-basin, multi-sectorally, taking into account surface and ground water for sustainable use incorporating quantity and quality aspects as well as environmental considerations. All indivi-dual developmental projects and proposals should be formulated and considered within the framework of such an overall plan keeping in view the existing agreements/awards for a basin or a sub-basin so that the best possible combination of options can be selected and sustained.

Watershed management through extensive soil construction, catchment-area treatment, preservation of forests and increasing the forest cover and the construc-tion of check-dams should be promoted. Efforts shall be to conserve the water in the catchment. Water should be made available to water short areas by transfer from other areas including transfers from one river basin to another, based on a national perspective, after taking into account the requirements of the areas/basins.

Institutional Mechanism

With a view to give effect to the planning, development and management of the water resources on a hydrological unit basis, along with a multi-sectoral multi-disciplinary and participatory approach as well as integrating quality, quantity and the environmental aspects, the existing institutions at various levels under the water resources sector will have to be appropriately reoriented/reorganized and even created, wherever necessary. As maintenance of water resource schemes is under non-plan budget, it is generally being neglected. The institutional arrangements should be such that this vital aspect is given importance equal or even more than that of new constructions.

Appropriate river basin organisations should be established for the planned development and manage-ment of a river basin as a hole or sub-basins, wherever necessary. Special multi-disciplinary units should be set up to prepare comprehensive plans taking into account not only the needs of irrigation but also harmonizing various other water uses, so that the available water resources are determined and opt to optimum use having regard to existing agreements or awards of Tribunals under the relevant laws. The scope and powers of the river basin organizations shall be decided by the basin states themselves.

Water Allocation Priorities

In the planning and operation of systems, water allocation priorities should be broadly as follows:

- Drinking water
- Irrigation
- Hydro-power
- Ecology
- Agro-industries and non-agricultural industries
- Navigation and other uses.

However, the priorities could be modified or added if warranted by the area/region specified considerations.

Project Planning

Water resource development projects should as far as possible be planned and developed as multipurpose projects. Provision for drinking water should be a primary consideration. The study of the likely impact of a project during construction and late on human lives, settlements, occupations, socio-economic, environment and other aspects shall form an essential component of project planning.

In the planning, implementation and operation of a project, the preservation of the quality of environment and the ecological balance should be a primary consideration The adverse impact on the environment, if any, should be minimized and should be offset by adequate compensatory measures. The project should. nevertheless, be sustainable.

Their should be an integrated and multi-disciplinary approach to the planning, formulation, clearance and implementation of projects, including catchment area treatment and management, environmental and ecological aspects, the rehabilitation of affected people and command area development. The planning of projects in hilly areas should take into account the need to provide assured drinking water, possibilities of hydro-power development and the proper approach to irrigation in such areas, in the context of physical features and constraints of the basin such as steep slopes, rapid run-off and the incidence of soil erosion. The economic evaluation of projects in such areas should also take these factors into account.

Special efforts should be made to investigate and formulate projects either in, or for the benefit of, areas inhabited by tribal or other specially disadvantaged groups such as socially weak, scheduled castes and scheduled tribes. In other areas also, project planning should pay special attention to the needs of scheduled castes and scheduled tribes and other weaker sections of the society. The economic evaluation of projects benefiting such disadvantaged sections should also take these factors into account. The drainage system should form an integral part of any irrigation project right from the planning stage.

Time and cost over-runs and deficient realization of benefits characterizing most water related projects should be overcome by upgrading the quality of project preparation and management. The inadequate funding of projects should be obviated by an optimal allocation of resources on the basis of prioritization, having regard to the early completion of on-going projects as well as the need to reduce regional imbalances. The involvement and participation of beneficiaries and other stakeholders should be encouraged right from the project planning stage itself.

Ground Water Development

There should be a periodical reassessment of the ground water potential on a scientific basis, Taking into consideration the quality of the water available and economic viability of its extraction.

Exploitation of ground water resources should be so regulated as not to exceed the recharging possibilities, as also to ensure social equality, the detrimental environ-mental consequences of over-exploitation of ground water need to be effectively prevented by the Central and State Governments. Ground water recharge projects should be developed and implemented for improving both the quality and availability of ground water resource.

Integrated and coordinated development of surface water and ground water resources and their conjunctive use, should be envisaged right from the project planning stage and should form an integral part of the project implementation. Over exploitation of ground water should be avoided especially near the coast to prevent ingress of sea water into sweet water aquifers.

Drinking Water

Adequate safe drinking water facilities should be provided to the entire population both in urban and in rural areas. Irrigation and multipurpose projects should invariably include a drinking water component, wherever there is no alternative source of drinking water. Drinking water needs of human beings and animals should be the first charge on any available water.

Irrigation

Irrigation planning either in an individual project or in a basin as a whole should take into account the irriga-bility of land, cost-effective irrigation options possible from all available sources of water and appropriate irrigation techniques for optimizing water use efficiency. Irrigation intensity should be such as to extend the benefits of irrigation to as large a number of farm families as possible, keeping in view the need to maximize production. There should be a close integration of water-use and land use policies.

Water allocation in an irrigation system should be done with due regard to equity and social justice. Disparities in the availability of water between head-reach and tail-end farms and between large and small farms should be obviated by adoption of a rational water distribution system and supply of water on a volumetric basis subject to certain ceilings and rational pricing.

Concerted efforts should be made to ensure that the irrigation potential created is fully utilized. For this purpose, the command area development approach should be adopted in all irrigation projects.

Irrigation being the largest consumer of fresh water, the aim should be to get optimal productivity per unit of water. Scientific water management, farm practices and sprinkler and drip system of irrigation should be adopted wherever feasible.

Reclamation of water logged/saline affected land by scientific and cost-effective methods should form a part of command area development programme.

Resettlement and Rehabilitation

Optimal use of water resources necessitates construc-tion of storages and the consequent resettlement and rehabilitation of population. A skeletal national policy in this regard needs to be formulated so that the project-affected persons share the benefits through proper rehabilitation. States should accordingly evolve their own detailed resettlement and rehabilitation policies for the sector, taking into account the local conditions. Careful planning is necessary to ensure that the construction and rehabilitation activities proceed simultaneously and smoothly.

Financial and Physical Sustainability

Besides creating additional water resources facilities for various uses, adequate emphasis needs to be given to the physical and financial sustainability of existing facilities. There is, therefore, a need to ensure that the water charges for various uses should be fixed in such a way that they cover at least the operation and maintenance charges of providing the service initially and a part of the capital costs subsequently. These rates should be linked directly to the quality of service provided. The subsidy on water rates to the disadvantaged and poorer sections of the society should be well targeted and transparent.

Participatory Approach to Water Resources Management

Management of the water resources for diverse uses should incoporate a participatory approach; by involving not only the various governmental agencies but also the users and other stakeholders, in an effective and decisive manner, in various aspects of planning, design, develop-ment and management of the water resources schemes. Necessary legal and institutional changes should be made at various levels for the purpose, duly ensuring appro-priate role for women. Water Users' Associations and the local bodies such as municipalities and gram panchayats should particularly be involved in the operation, mainte-nance and management of water infrastructures/facilities at appropriate levels progressively, with a view to eventually transfer the management of such facilities to the user groups/local bodies.

Private Sector Participation

Private sector participation should be encouraged in planning, development and management of water resources projects for diverse uses, wherever feasible. Private sector participation may help in introducing innovative ideas, generating financial resources and introducing corporate management and improving service efficiency and accountability to users. Depending upon the specific situations, various combinations of private sector participation, in building, owning, operating, leasing and transferring of water resources facilities, may be considered.

Water Quality

Both surface water and ground water should be regularly monitored for quality. A phased programme should be undertaken for improvements in water quality. Effluents should be treated to acceptable levels and standards before discharging them into natural streams. Minimum flow should be ensured in the perennial streams for maintaining ecology and social considerations.

Principle of 'polluter pays' should be followed in management of polluted water. Necessary legislation is to be made for preservation of existing water bodies by preventing encroachment and deterioration of water quality.

Water Zoning

Economic development and activities including agricultural, industrial and urban development, should be planned with due regard to the constraints imposed by the configuration of water availability. There should be a water zoning of the country and the economic activities should be guided and regulated in accordance with such zoning.

Conservation of Water

Efficiency of utilization in all the diverse uses of water should be optimized and an awareness of water as a scarce resource should be fostered. Conservation consciousness should be promoted through education, regulation, incentives and disincentives.

The resources should be conserved and the availability augmented by maximizing retention, eliminating pollution and minimizing losses. For this, measures like selective linings in the conveyance system, modernization and rehabilitation of existing systems including tanks, recycling and refuse of treated effluents and adoption of traditional techniques like mulching or pitcher irrigation and new techniques like drip and sprinkler may be promoted, wherever feasible.

Flood Control and Management

There should be a master plan for flood control and manage-ment for each flood prone basin. Adequate flood-cushion should be provided in water storage projects, wherever feasible, to facilitate better flood management. In highly flood prone areas, flood control should be given overriding consideration in reservoir regulation policy even at the cost of sacrificing some irrigation or power benefits.

While physical flood protection works like embank-ments and dykes will continue to be necessary, increased emphasis should be laid on non-structural measures such as flood forecasting and warning, flood plain zoning and flood proofing for the minimization of losses and to reduce the recurring expenditure on flood relief.

There should be strict regulation of settlements and economic activity in the flood plain zones along with flood proofing, to minimize the loss of life and property on account of floods. The flood forecasting activities should be modernized, value added and extended to other uncovered areas. Inflow forecasting to reservoirs should be instituted for their effective regulation.

Land Erosion by Sea or River

The erosion of land, whether by the sea in coastal areas or by river waters inland, should be minimized by stable cost-effective measures. The States and Union Territories should also undertake all requisite steps to ensure that indiscriminate occupation and exploitation of coastal strips of land are discouraged and that the location of economic activities in areas adjacent to the sea is regulated.

Each coastal State should prepare a comprehensive coastal land management plan, keeping in view the environmental and ecological impacts, and regulate the developmental activities accordingly.

Drought-prone Area Development

Drough-prone Areas should be made less vulnerable to drought-associated problems through soil-moisture conservation measures, water harvesting practices, minimization of evaporation losses, development of the ground water potential including recharging and the transfer of surface water from surplus areas where feasible and appropriate. Pastures, forestry or other modes of development which are relatively less water demanding should be encouraged. In planning water resource development projects, the needs of drught-prone areas should be given priority. Relief works undertaken for providing employment to drought-stricken population should preferably be for drought proofing.

Monitoring of Projects

A close monitoring of projects to identify bottlenecks and to adopt timely measures to obviate time and cost overrun should form part of project planning and execution.

There should be a system to monitor and evaluate the performance and socio-economic impact of the project.

Water Sharing/Distribution amongst the States

The water sharing and distribution amongst the states should be guided by a national perspective with due regard to water resources availability and need within the river basin. Necessary guidelines, including for water short states even outside the basin, need to be evolved for facilitating future agreements amongst the basin states.

The Inter-State Water Disputes Act of 1956 may be suitably reviewed and amended for timely adjudication of water disputes referred to the Tribunal.

Performance Improvement

There is an urgent need of paradigm shift in the emphasis in the management of water resources sector. From the present emphasis on the creation and expansion of water resources infrastructures for diverse uses, there is now a need to give greater emphasis on the improve-ment of the performance of the existing water resources facilities. Therefore, allocation of funds under the water resources sector should be re-priorities to ensure that the needs for development as well as operation and maintenance of the facilities are met.

Maintenance and Modernization

Structures and systems created through massive investments should be properly maintained in good health. Appropriate annual provisions should be made for this purpose in the budgets.

There should be a regular monitoring the structures and systems and necessary rehabilitation and moderni-zation programmes should be undertaken.

Formation of Water Users' Association with authority and responsibility should be encouraged to facilitate the management including maintenance of irrigation system in a time bound manner.

Safety of Structures

There should be proper organizational arrangements at the national and state levels for ensuring the safety of storage dams and other water-related structures consisting of specialists in investigation, design, construction, hydrology, geology, etc. A dam safety legislation may be enacted to ensure proper inspection, maintenance and surveillance of existing dams and also to ensure proper planning, investigation, designs and construction for safety of new dams. The Guidelines on the subject should be periodically updated and reformulated. There should be a system of continuous surveillance and regular visits by experts.

Science and Technology

For effective and economical management of our water resources, the frontiers of knowledge need to be pushed forward in several directions by intensifying research efforts in various areas, including the following:

- Hydrometeorology;
- Snow and lake hydrology;
- Surface and ground water hydrology;
- River morphology and hydraulics;
- Assessment of water resources;
- Water harvesting and ground water recharge;
- Water quality;
- Water conservation;
- Evaporation and seepage losses;
- Recycling and re-use;
- Better water management practices and improvements in operational technology;

- Crops and cropping systems;
- Soils and material research;
- New construction materials and technology (with particular reference to roller compacted concrete, fibre reinforced concrete, new metho-dologies in tunneling technologies, instrumen-tation, advanced numerical analysis instructures and back analysis);
- Seismology and seismic design of structures;
- The safety and longevity of water-related struc-tures;
- Economical designs for water resource projects;
- Risk analysis and disaster management;
- Use of remote sensing techniques in develop-ment and management;
- Use of static ground water resource as a crisis management measure;
- Sedimentation of reservoirs;
- Use of sea water resources;
- Prevention of Salinity ingress;
- Prevention of water logging and soil salinity;
- Reclamation of Water logged and saline lands;
- Environmental impact;
- Regional equity;

Training

A perspective plan for standardized training should be an integral part of water resource development. It should cover training in information systems, sectoral planning, project planning and formulation, project management, operation of projects and their physical structures and systems and the management of the water distribution systems. The training should extend to all the categories of personnel involved in these activities as also the farmers.

Conclusion

In view of the vital importance of water for human and animal life, for maintaining economic and developmental activities of all kinds, and considering its increasing scarcity, the planning and management of this resource and its optimal, economical and equitable use has become a matter of the utmost urgency. Concerns of the community needs to be taken into account for water resources development and management. The success of the National Water Policy will depend entirely on evolving and maintaining a national consensus and commitment to its underlying principles and objectives. To achieve the desired objectives, State Water Policy backed with an operational action plan shall be formulated in a time bound manner say in two years. National Water Policy may be revised periodically as and when need arises.

Appendix-IV

Milestone dates/time Table for interlinking of Rivers

(i)	Notification of the Task Force	By *16-12-2002*
(ii)	Preparation of Action Plan-I, giving an outline of the time schedules for the completion of the feasibility studies, detailed project reports, estimated cost. Implementation schedule, concrete benefits and advantages of the project, etc.	39-04-2003
(iii)	Preparation of Action Plan-II, giving alternative options for funding and execution of the project as also the suggested methods for cost recovery.	31-07-2003
(iv)	Meeting with the Chief Ministers to deliberate over the project and to elicit their cooperation.	May/June, 2003
(v)	Completion of Feasibility Studies (already in progress).	31-12-2005
(vi)	Completion of Detailed Project Reports. (Preparation of DPRs will start simultaneouly since FSs in respect of six river links have already been completed).	31-12-2006
(vii)	Implementation of the Project (10 years).	31-12-2016

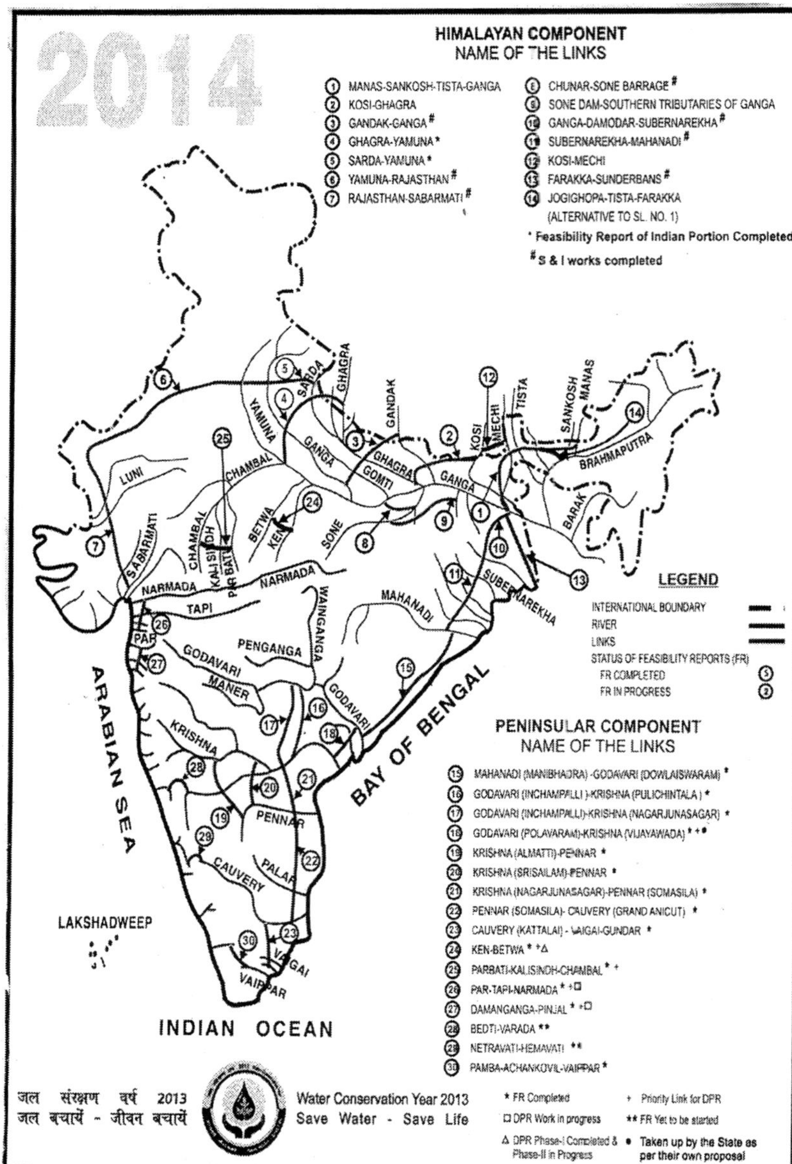

Courtsey—National Water Development Agency

References

1. Association of Hydrologists of India, 2003, Proceedings of National Conference on "Interlinking of Indian Rivers", Visakhapatnam, Special Issue of Journal of Applied Hydrology, Association of Hydiologists of India, 2003.
2. Central Water Commission, 2000 'River V Allye Projects and Environment-Concerns and Management', Publication No. 61/2000, New Delhi, December 2000.
3. Centre for Science and Environment, "Floods, Flood Plains and Environmental Myths-State of India's Environment-A Citizens, Report", Centre for Science and Environment, New Delhi 1991.
4. Central Electricity Authority, 1991, 'Perspective of National Power Plan Development upto 2006-07' New Delhi.
5. Central Water Commission. 1988, 'Water Resources of India', New Delhi.
6. Central Water Commission, 1992, 'Guidelines for Sustainable Water Resources Development and Management', New Delhi.
7. Confederation of Indian Industries, 2003, Proceedings of Discussion on "Interlinking of Indian Rivers", New Delhi, February 2003.
8. Dahasahasara S.V, Katpatal Y.B. and Mahajan M.M. 2004, 'National River-Linking', Civil

Engineering & construction Review, Journal, May 2004.

9. Dhawan B.D. 1999, 'Studies in Indian Irrigation', Commonwealth Publishers, New Delhi.
10. FICCI, 2003, Proceedings of National conference on "Interlinking of Indian Rivers", New Delhi, March 2003.
11. Goel R.S. (Editor), 2000, "Environmental Management in Hydropower and River Valley Projects - Techniques of Management, Policy Issues, Case Studies and Application of Scientific Tools', ISBN-81-204-1423-3, MIS Oxford & IBH Publishing Co. Pvt. Ltd., New Delhi.
12. Goel R. S. and Srivastva R.N. (Editors), 2000, "Hydropower and River Valley Development-Environment Management, Case Studies and Policy Issues", MIS Oxford & IBH Publishing Co. Ltd., New Delhi.
13. India Water Partnership, 2000, "India Water Vision 2025-Report of The Vision Development Consultation", New Delhi.
14. Indian Water Resources Society, 2000, "Theme Paper on Human Issues Involved in Water Resoures Development", New Delhi.
15. Indian Water Resources Society, 2009, "Special Issue of Journal of Indian Water Resources Society Containing Dr. Kanwar Sain memorial Lectures", ISSN 0970-6984, Roorkee.
16. Indian Water Resources Society, 2001, "Theme Paper on Management of Floods and Droughts", New Delhi.
17. Indian Water Resources Society, 2002, "Theme

Paper on Integrated Water Resources Development & Management", New Delhi.

18. Jayant B. and Shama P., "Interlinking of Rivers in India -Asessing the Justifications", Paper presented at Discussion on Interlinking of Rivers, The Institution of Engineers (India), West Bengal State Centre, Sept.r 04.
19. Joshi P.K., "Environmental Impacts Assessment of Irrigation Projects", Seminar on Irrigation Water management, Water Management Forum, New Delhi, 1992.
20. Mahendra Engineering College, 2003, Proceedings of National Conference on "Interlinking of Indian Rivers - Problems and Perspectives", Mahendrapuri, Namakkal, Tamilnadu, August 2003.
21. Ministry of Health and Family Welfare, 1995, "Report of National Mission on Environmental Health and Sanitation', New Delhi.
22. Ministry of Water Resources, 1999, Report of the National Commission for Integrated Water Resources Development, New Delhi.
23. Ministry of Water Resources, 2001, Report of the Working Group on Water Related Ecological Matters for X Five Year Plan, New Delhi.
24. Minister of Water Resources, 2001, "Report of the Working Group on Major and Medium Irrigation Programme for X Five Year Plan", New Delhi.
25. Ministry of Water Resources, 2001, "Report of the Working Group on Flood Control Programme for X Five Year Plan", New Delhi.
26. Ministry of Water Resources, 2003, Vision for Integrated Water Resources Development and Management, New Delhi.

27. Ministry of Water Resources, 2003, 'Interbasin Water Transfer Proposals', New Delhi.
28. Ministry of Power, 1999, "Hydro Power Policy", New Delhi.
29. Prasad Kamta and Goel R.S. (Editors), 2000, Environmental Management in Hydro Electric Projects', ISBN-81-7022-870-0, MIS Concept Publishing Company, New Delhi.
30. Planning Commission, 1996, "Report of the Working Group on Urban Water Supply and Sanitation Sector for IX Five Year Plan", New Delhi.
31. Supreme Court Judgement, 2000, Narmada Bahao Andolan Vs. Union of India, AIR, SCC, 2000.
32. Water Management Forum, 2002, 'Theme Paper on Inter-Basin Transfers of Water–Challenges and Oppoutunities', New Delhi.
33. Yojana–Water Management Spl. June 2005-Radhakant Bharati–Interlinking of Rivers.
34. Arvindo Ghosh–Kurukshetra (Govt. of India Publication), New Delhi.
35. Journal of Indian Instt. of Public Admn., New Delhi. 2011-12 & 13.
36. Bhagirath Journals (English & Hindi) Publication of M/o Water Resources, New Delhi 2011 & 12.
37. India Year Book, 2014, Publication Division.
38. Seminar on ILR, C.B.I. & P., New Delhi.
39. Modern Temples of India–R.K. Bharati, National Book Trust, New Delhi.
40. Report of N.W.D.A. an I.L.R. by D.G., A.B. Pandya.
41. Supreme Courts Directions on I.L.R. 2012.
42. Immortal India–J.H. Dave, Vidya Bhavan Publication

Maps & Diagrams

View of Tehri Dam
on
River Ganga

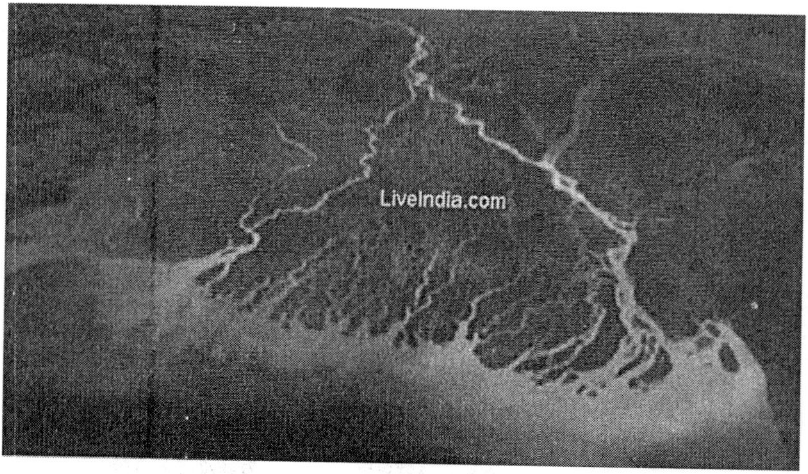

Aerial View of Sunderbans Delta

View of Sardar Sarover Dam on Narmada

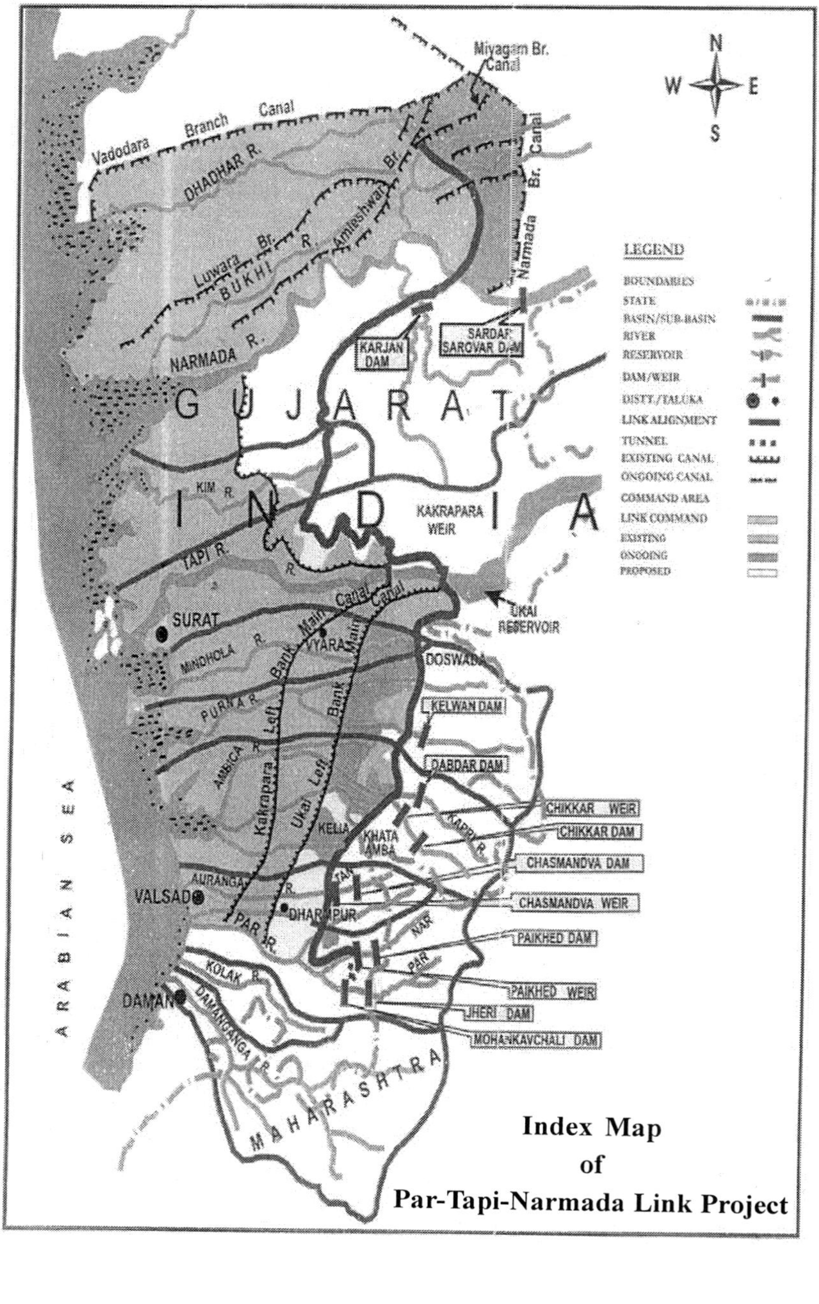

Index Map of Par-Tapi-Narmada Link Project